Guide for Logo and

Trademark Drawings

Graphic Requirements of the USPTO and WIPO's Madrid International Trademark System

Studio 94 S.M.
PUBLISHING

Written & Illustrated by
Murray H. Henderson

Guide for Logo & Trademark Drawings
ISBN-13: 978-0-9828270-4-8
ISBN-10: 0-9828270-4-0

Dedication

To my late wife,
Evelyn Ryder Henderson,
for her creative graphic designs
and strong work ethic

ACKNOWLEDGMENTS
I would like to thank the following people for their assistance,
suggestions, remarks and reviews on this book,
and of special interest during my research:
The Oppedahl Patent Law Firm LLC. sponsors of email discussion groups for
practitioners in trademarks, patents, copyrights, Patent Cooperation Treaty,
Madrid Protocol, and industrial designs and Macs in Law Offices (MILO);
(I am a fly on the wall observing attorney problem areas);
and to all those creative people I have had the gratification of assisting
with their inventions and start-up businesses, with something
as simple as a new type of paper clip to the
technology that helped get us to the moon.

*The author is not affiliated with, nor is he endorsed by,
the United States Patent and Trademark Office (USPTO)
or by the World Intellectual Property Organization (WIPO).*

i

Logos and trademarks on the cover

Water Gypsy Picnic Sails: Evelyn Henderson

Friendly Dog: Rod Kam

Class design 99: Murray Henderson

The WOW Company: Evelyn Henderson

Scott Hawaii: Evelyn Henderson

The famous "Ford Blue Oval" is a good example
of a mark that is known worldwide.
The main character of the script "Ford" has not changed
much in 92 years. The Ford Trademark was first registered in 1928
as a black & white design and changed to blue in 1961.
To illustrate its value, the Ford Motor Company in 2006
used it and other North American Ford assets as collateral
in securing a line of credit for $23.5 billion.

CONTENTS

CONTENTS

CONTENTS

CONTENTS

CONTENTS

CONTENTS

Chapter 1

Introduction, definition of Trademarks,
Logos, Brand Names and Trade Dress.
Author's background and the
start of Studio 94.

Reproducibility of Graphic Images

People working with graphics soon learn the various techniques and rules that make for good graphic reproductions. I have observed artists who are good at creative work, but are not very good at the technical aspects of reproduction of their creative work, kind of a right-brain/left-brain thing.

This is why my wife, Evelyn Ryder Henderson, and I made a good graphics team; she was good at creative design, and I made it work for reproduction. In successful graphic design shops, good designs are generally a team effort. On many occasions I was given a newly-designed corporate logo that had reproduction problems and was instructed to fix it– *"make it reproduce well for our various media applications."*

Trademarks, one of the oldest forms of Intellectual Property

Trademark Drawings can be produced with a variety of graphic techniques with more latitude than any of the other form of intellectual property drawings. The trademark graphic image can be produced in a variety of ways by using almost any medium such as: hand sketching, black ink, paint colors; airbrushing, block printing, silk screening, photography, and even embroidery or needlepoint images and/or by using various computer software applications that will produce a USPTO and WIPO approved image.

Trademark drawings have very few rules as long as the drawing image is within the size limitations and can produce a quality image, electronic and/or on paper, and can be displayed on your goods or services.

> The depiction of the mark you submit now is what will appear on your registration certificate once the application process is completed.
> And remember: You cannot add or subtract words and designs to the mark throughout the process, except in very rare circumstances.
> So, the mark you submit now is what will register later.
> And you want it to look perfect, right?
> *Source: USPTO Video instructions*

Introduction

Trademarks, Logos and Business Brands

Trademarks and Business Branding are the most valuable pieces of Intellectual Property you can own. Registered trademarks that are kept up to date and registration fees paid, can go on as long as the owner of the mark is in business, whereas a *design patent or design registration* only lasts about 15 years.

Good corporate identification designs (logo/trademark/trade dress) involves many hours of research, collaboration with the company's management, marketing and legal departments. The corporate design involves experimenting with colors, using words and images that are internationally accepted, and then creating a graphic image that has instant public recognition, close-up and at a distance.

A classic example is the Nike *"Swoosh"* a corporate trademark created in 1971 by Carolyn Davidson, while she was a graphic design student at Portland State University. In June 1972, the first running shoes bearing the *Swoosh* were introduced at the U.S. Track and Field Olympic Trials in Eugene, Oregon. Until 1995, the official corporate logo for Nike featured the name Nike in Futura Bold, all-cap font, cradled within the Swoosh. In 1995, Nike began using the stand-alone Swoosh as its corporate logo, and continues to use it that way today.   *Source: Wikipedia.*

Classic training for graphic design students generally involved a study of how their design appears on a business card, package and on a side of a truck. The test was to see if the design was legible at these various sizes. Today with new technology the design image must also be tested to see how legible it is on digital screens: smart phones, graphic tablets, monitors and large screen HD video.

After a design is approved, the designer typically produces printed specifications on "how the corporate design (trademark) must be used." These specifications are generally done under the guidance of the client's legal department and generally contain "camera-ready, or digital-ready copies of the logo/trademark" and instructions for printers and others on how the logo/trademark must to be used. Without these specifications, others may change your specified color, type style, and sometimes the graphic itself, putting the corporate identity in legal jeopardy.

As Jimmy Durante often said–
"Everybody wants to get inta the act."

Logo Definition: "A logo is a graphic mark or emblem commonly used by commercial enterprises, organizations and even individuals to aid and promote instant public recognition. Logos are either purely graphic (symbols/icons) or are composed of the name of the organization (a logotype or word-mark).

In the days of hot metal typesetting, a logotype was a uniquely set and arranged typeface or colophon. At the level of mass communication and in common usage, a company's logo is today often synonymous with its trademark or brand.

Logo design is an important area of graphic design, and one of the most difficult to perfect. The logo (ideogram), is the image embodying an organization. Because logos are meant to represent companies' brands or corporate identities and foster their immediate customer recognition, *it is counterproductive to frequently redesign logos."*

Source: Wikipedia.

The Value of Good Design

"Design contributes in many important ways to the UK economy; in fact £33.5 billion was invested in design in 2008, which is 2.4% of GDP. The UK boasts some of the world's best designers across a range of both expected and unexpected industries, from fashion to automotive, furniture to high tech, food products to engineering."

Source: Call for Evidence Design, Intellectual Property Office UK
Website: www.ipo.gov.uk

AUTHOR'S COMMENTS

In 1985, my wife Evelyn and I made a business/vacation trip to London. We were invited to an Industries Design Trade Show in Kensington and both of us were very impressed with the quality of the designs.

A lot of our clients in the travel industry, real estate development and new business start-ups brought in rough-stage logo designs that were very creative but needed to be put into a working logos and/or trademarks that could be reproduced for print and for USPTO Trademark applications.

Guide for Logo and Trademark Drawings is a brief and to the point reference manual that incorporates areas covered in the various USPTO and WIPO Madrid International Trademark System rules regarding trademark drawings and reproductions, and is a result of the author's many years of experience working with IP attorneys, agents, engineers, inventors, scientists and entrepreneurs by illustrating their inventions, trademarks and their business startup items such as business cards, letterhead, envelopes, company logos, technical manuals and illustrations for grant programs.

AUTHOR'S COMMENTS
I have included only the rules from the October, 2018 TMEP
(Trademark Manual of Examination Procedure) that
involve drawings and reproductions and the digital image files
for electronic submittal to the USPTO and WIPO
(World Intellectual Property Organization)
Madrid International Trademark System.
All other legal Information you will find in the USPTO's TMEP manual.

What's the difference between trademark and patent drawings?
Patent drawings have specific rules about how they are done and how they must comply for digital image applications, whereas trademark drawings have no rules about how the drawings are done, only rules on their digital submission requirements and will the mark reproduce clearly.

What's the difference between a logo and a trademark?
A trademark protects a slogan, phrase, word(s), company name, logo, or design that identifies a company and/or its goods. A logo is a symbol or design used by a company that may fall under trademark protection laws. Logos are not always just a symbol or design, sometimes they are a melding of font letters (Ligatures). In fact, logos started out that way and they were called "logo-type."

A good example of a ligature logo
The CNN logo has earned a wonderful reputation in the corporate world due to its powerful and timeless design. The logo was designed by the noted graphic artist Anthony Guy Bost in 1980 for a reported fee of $2,800. Since then, the emblem has largely remained unchanged.

Source: Famous Logos

Many of the most successful companies in the U.S. have instantly recognizable logos. Example, you could show the Nike "swoosh" to almost anyone in the world and they know immediately what brand it represents.

What is the difference between brand and trademark?
There is a legal difference between the two words. A trademark is a mark that legally represents something, usually a business, by their goods or services. A brand name, however, is the name that a business chooses for one of its products. Brand names can also be trademarked and/or be in the trade dress category.

It is important to understand whether you should file for a trademark/service mark, a patent, and/or a copyright. While all are types of intellectual property, each protects something very specific. USPTO.
Another aspect is to look at is the length of time each IP protects your creation.

A question I was frequently asked–
"On what products do you see the most intellectual property?"
MHH: *On food packaging especially frozen foods. First the package resulted from a utility and/or design patent then the package is imprinted with 3 or 4 trademarks; the food company, the brand, a third-party diet company and finally a TM for recycling the package, it also includes copyrighted food photos and text.*
And also the packaging may be protected by Trade Dress.
All of that in your freezer!

What is Trade Dress?
Trade dress is the characteristics of the visual appearance of a product or its packaging or even the design of a building that signify the source of the product to consumers. Examples of trade dress: The book jackets of *For Dummies* books and the *Take Control* Books; the design of Apple Stores; a similarity design of an airline's booking area, uniforms, documents, web-site and the aircraft decorative design inside and exterior.

Drawing of your "Special Form" mark
Your application must include a clear "drawing" or depiction of the trademark you want to register. We also call a "drawing" a "mark drawing" or a "representation of the mark." Federal trademark law requires that you provide a drawing with your application for us to assign the application a filing date and move it toward registration.

How are drawings used?
Once your application has a filing date, we upload the drawing of your trademark into our automated records. The public can view these records online using the Trademark Electronic Search System (TESS) and the Trademark Status and Document Retrieval (TSDR) databases. This publicly available information about your trademark may help you avoid subsequent legal conflicts.

The trademark that appears in your drawing will also appear on your registration
certificate.   Source: USPTO

Which type of drawing should I use?

Which type of drawing should I use and which provides broader protection?
This decision depends on many factors, including the mark you use most often with your goods or services, which words or designs are important for you to protect, and how much money you plan to spend on protecting the mark.

For example, companies often separately register various components of a mark that they use together and separately. A company might register its business name, a slogan, and a logo to ensure the broadest possible protection. This gives companies flexibility in their promotional matter, social media, and webpages to mix and match marks (sometimes using a slogan or design alone, or a design with the slogan) and still protect all their marks.

Some companies, however, can afford to register only one mark, so they might focus instead on registering the one or two components they use most often and that are most important to their brand. Because this decision is important, an applicant may wish to hire a private attorney specializing in trademark matters.

Do I have to register my mark?

Although federal registration of a mark is not mandatory, it has several advantages, including notice to the public of the registrant's claim of ownership of the mark, legal presumption of ownership nationwide, and exclusive right to use the mark on or in connection with the goods/services listed in the registration. USPTO.

To submit a new mark drawing

The instructions presume that you will use a TEAS form to respond online to more than one issue. To respond using TEAS, fill out the form to address all issues in the office action and, at the end of the form, the correct party must properly sign it. It is important that the proper party sign your response, otherwise we may not accept it and you could miss the deadline for responding to an office action. For more information about who may sign a response, please review your office action.

1. If you are responding to a **nonfinal office action,** use the **Response to Examining Attorney Office Action form.** If you are responding to a **final office action,** use the **Request for Reconsideration after Final Action form.**

2. Answer "Yes" to question 4 on the form.

3. In the "Mark Information" section of the form, check the box stating that you have read and understood that a material alteration will not be permitted.

4. To amend your mark, do the following:

    a. For a standard character mark (non-stylized text mark), click the box by "Standard Characters" and type the new mark in the text field for adding/modifying the standard character mark.

    b. For a special form mark:

i. Click the box for "Special Form (Stylized and/or Design)."

ii. Click the "Browse" button to select a JPG image file from your local drive; the image size cannot exceed 5 megabytes. (If you are claiming color as a feature of the mark, you must submit a color image.)

iii. Click the "Open" file button.

iv. After the file name appears in the window, click the "Attach" button to upload the file into the application.

v. Enter the literal elements in the text field below.

vi. Enter further below a complete description of all text and/or design elements in the text field for a mark description.

5. If your mark is in color, after you click the box for "Special Form (Stylized and/or Design)" enter each color appearing in the mark in the field for claiming color and revise the mark description to indicate where color is located in the mark.

File format and size requirements for special form mark images
• JPG file format
• File size is 5 megabytes or smaller
• File name is less than 256 characters, including ".jpg" file extension
• Zipped or compressed files are not acceptable
• Mark image has as little white space as possible around the design
• If a color mark, use RGB color scheme; if you can open your image with your browser, then it is saved in the RGB color scheme. Do not use the CMYK color scheme when using design programs such as Adobe Photoshop or Illustrator.

Recommendations for creating high-quality images with a scanner
Scanning is not recommended. If you must scan:
• Scan a high-quality original
• Use software to crop, resize, and adjust the image to minimize white space around the design
• For black and white or color images, ensure dots per inch (DPI) of 300-350, and pixel range of 250-944 for both length and width
• For grayscale images, ensure 8 bits per sample pixel. We consider grayscale images to be black and white. (See pages 32 and 33).

Drawing requirements for unusual marks
• 3D marks and trademark trade dress (3D product design or product packaging), or service mark trade dress – you generally need to provide a special form drawing showing a single rendition of your mark in three dimensions.

• Motion marks – you must provide a special form drawing showing a single point in the movement, or a square showing up to five freeze frames of various points in the movement of your mark.

• **Scent marks** – you must provide a standard character drawing with "scent mark" typed as the mark.

• **Sound marks** – you must select "sound mark" as your mark type. You must then submit the actual sound of the sound mark in a .wav, .wmv, .wma, .mp3, or .avi format that does not exceed 5 megabytes in size.

We also require a detailed written description for these unusual marks because the mark drawing cannot always adequately represent them. For 3D and trade dress marks, you must mention in your description that the mark is three-dimensional. For more information about drawings for these types of marks, see TMEP §807.09 (for sound, scent, and non-visual marks), TMEP §807.10 and TMEP §1202.02(c)(i) (for 3D and trade dress marks), and TMEP §807.11 (for motion marks).

Other initial considerations

Before starting the application process, it is important to have clearly in mind (1) the mark you want to register; (2) the goods and/or services in connection with which you wish to register the mark; and (3) whether you will be filing the application based on actual existing use of the mark or a bona fide intention to use the mark in the future. This will make your search of the USTPO database more useful and may simplify the application process. More details on mark types, goods and services, filing basis, and searching are provided in the next four sections.

Identifying your mark: Select one of three possible formats

An important consideration is the depiction of your mark. Every application must include a clear representation of the mark you want to register. We use this representation (1) to file the mark in the USPTO search records and to (2) print the mark in the Official Gazette (OG) and (3) on the registration certificate. The OG, a weekly on-line publication, gives notice to the public that the USPTO plans to issue a registration.

Identifying your goods and/or services

Once you have chosen your mark, you must also be able to identify the goods and/or services to which the mark will apply, clearly and precisely. The identification of goods and/or services must be specific enough to identify the nature of the goods and/or services. The level of specificity depends on the type of goods and/or services. For examples of acceptable identifications, please consult the **Acceptable Identification of Goods and Services Manual (ID Manual).**

NOTE:
Under U.S. Trademark law, class headings from the
International Schedule of Classes of Goods and Services
by themselves are not acceptable for registration purposes.
The specific items of goods and/ or services must be listed.

Searching marks in USPTO database

You should **search the USPTO database** before filing your application, to determine whether anyone already claims trademark rights in a particular mark through a federal registration. Failure to conduct a proper search may result in your not making a proper assessment as to whether an application should even be filed. I would also highly recommend a search of your State and WIPO's Madrid Global Brand Database.

Filing a Trademark application

You may **file your trademark application on-line** using the Trademark Electronic Application System (TEAS). USPTO.

Protecting your rights

You are responsible for enforcing your rights if you receive a registration, because the USPTO does not "police" the use of marks. While the USPTO attempts to ensure that no other party receives a federal registration for an identical or similar mark for or as applied to related goods/services, the owner of a registration is responsible for bringing any legal action to stop a party from using an infringing mark.

Trademark manual of examining procedure (TMEP)

For additional information on various topics, you may also wish to consult another USPTO electronic resource, the
Trademark Manual of Examining Procedure (TMEP).
The TMEP provides trademark examining attorneys in the USPTO, trademark applicants, and attorneys and representatives for trademark applicants with a reference work on the current law, practices, and procedures relative to the federal trademark application and registration process. The TMEP contains information and guidelines designed to assist USPTO examining attorneys in reviewing trademark application. This information also may be useful to an applicant to better understand the trademark application process. The TMEP includes an **alphabetical index** by subject matter to help users locate pertinent information.

```
AUTHOR'S COMMENTS
See Chapter 3 for the rules in the TMEP that mostly
effect the trademark drawings, specimens, image
naming and file types.
```

About the Author

Murray Henderson is a graduate of Cooper School of Art, and attended Cleveland State University, Hawaii Pacific University and the University of Hawaii.

Henderson served eight years in the U.S. Navy Reserve as an Aircraft Torpedo man. He is a retired Technical Illustrator. He has worked for the NASA John Glenn Research Center, Cleveland, Ohio; NASA Langley Research Center, Virginia; Borg Warner and its Research Center, Chicago; Studio 94 Designing Woman Ltd. (his own graphic design studio in Honolulu operated with his wife, the late Evelyn Ryder Henderson).

He is Past President of Technology Enhancement Ltd. Hawaii; and Past President of The Inventors Connection of Greater Cleveland, a nonprofit corporation assisting independent inventors.

He has more than five decades of experience in patent and trademark drawings along with the graphics needed for business startups for inventors and intellectual property attorneys.

Henderson held a U.S. Government Secret Clearance from 1953 through 1974 on a need-to-know basis.

Author's background

After graduating from Cooper school of Art in 1953 I was hired by the Pesco Products Division of the Borg-Warner Corporation where I worked in engineering until the technical illustrator retired from the advertising and technical publishing department. The ad & tech department consisted of 17 employees and our work was divided about 50/50 between business advertising and military manuals mostly for the U.S. Air Force and NATO. My job was to illustrate exploded views and related drawings for Service Manuals and Parts Catalogs. It was at this time I was given my first Security Clearance on a "need to know basis" and my start in illustrating patent drawings for their Office of Patent Council.

The Value of a good invention

Pesco (Pump Engineering Service Co.) was the results of an invention for pressure loading gear pumps that led to the creation of a company that at its peak had 5,000 employees.

I have been interviewed at various times about inventions and patent drawings and one question that was always asked–
"What is your analysis of a good invention?"
In my opinion a good invention is one the creates commerce and it employs many.

Good training

My ten-years at Pesco gave me a good background in all aspects of the work; part advertising and part technical and because we were a small department I would have to help out in; tech writing, photography, printing, publishing and display shows for the U.S. Air Force. I also worked on classified projects at the Borg-Warner Research Center in Chicago. I resigned from Pesco after ten years to join NASA but in between I had a temporary job working on a classified U.S. Navy project for Goodyear Aircraft in Akron, Ohio.

A good time to work for NASA, we went to the moon!

NASA Lewis Research Center, Cleveland, Ohio (Now the John Glenn Research Ctr.)
I was hired to replace the retiring Section Head of the. Scientific Illustration Department that produced the drawings required for the engineers and scientists in publication of their research findings, patent drawings, presentation slides and animation for NASA video demonstrations. My security clearance was upgraded to Secret.

I was also assigned to work at the NASA Plum Brook Station, NASA Langley Research Center and sent on business trips to NASA Headquarters in Washington, D.C., NASA Ames Research Center, Moffett Field and the Jet Propulsion Laboratory, Pasadena, California.

Another part of my job was keeping track of 12,000 illustrations that at that time, it took literally days to locate drawings. In 1970 I became interested in computer science and took all the NASA classes I could take and I created a computer file system that married 3 different NASA scientific classes into one program and by working nights, myself and two others were able to record the 12,000 illustration records on key punch cards. This was before desktop computers.

A manual to go along with the computer process

I wrote and illustrated a technical manual about how to record and classify the various illustrations, and soon after one of our scientists came to my office and said,
"I'm in charge of our new aircraft and spacecraft safety program and I have a satellite up there right now to accept safety data but I don't at the present time have the data to test my satellite. I hear you have 12,000 keypunch cards with data on them. Can I borrow your cards to test my system?" (This was shortly after 3 astronauts died).
Yes, you can!
"You understand this will only be until I receive my safety data?"'
Yes, I understand.
Well, for a month I could go down the hall to the engineer's conference room and use a very upscale HP scientific calculator and search for specific drawings. I invited my boss to a demonstration and he was thrilled but I did not tell him it was bouncing up-and-down from a satellite or he would have imploded.

Move to Hawaii in January 1994

I resigned my job at NASA after ten years and my wife and I moved to Honolulu, Hawaii in 1974. My wife was hired by the Hawaii Newspaper Agency as an illustrator in the promotion department and I free lanced out of our apartment. This soon evolved into our own business that we named Studio 94 after our apartment number, 94.

Studio 94 the Graphics Design Shop

Between my wife's graphic designs, my technical illustrations and patent drawings, the free lance business brought in an enough business to rent our own office. We made a good team. With her creative skills and my technical abilities we made things work and soon hired additional artists.

Creating client's logos/trademarks

Our clients generally come in two basic categories: (1) they knew what they wanted with the main details but they needed us to create the graphic, or (2) they didn't know what they wanted and wanted us to create a logo/trademark and give them three samples.

Working with clients

The way we worked was to first, do a search on their proposed business name. This was easy, just go down to 1010 Richard's Street, just 10-minutes away from our office and look at the IBM print outs of all the Hawaii State registered business and trade names.

Note: when you live in Honolulu everyone wants to name their business Honolulu ..., Hawaii ..., Diamond Head ... or Pacific ... We would tell them to look through the Yellow Pages at all the related names and that would generally discourage them.

Back to our two basic category clients

Client one-They know what they want, we do their final logo/trademark and we work with an "Assignment of copyright," so they own it.

Client two-They don't know what they want and we come up with three logos, from there it generally goes two ways: (1) they chose one and it is theirs, copyright-free, or (2) they hate them all and refuse to pay. At this point if the graphics do not have their name on it, we keep them and they are ours.

From inventions to a business

A lot of the independent inventors I did patent drawings for, started a business that required a logo/trademark, business graphics, signage, etc. and after their business was up and running and they had free cash flow, they generally came up with improvements or additional inventions.

Example of one very successful business

Verifone. In the early 1980s I was asked to do design patent drawings of one of their first credit card verification terminals and that led to illustrating all the drawings required for their installation and service manuals. Through the 1980s untill I left Hawaii in 1994, Verifone's creative people came up with a new device about every month. The only drawings I did not do for them at that time was their trademark, but I was asked to make up their "mark clip-art-type sheets" with a range of the mark's sizes and to convert the mark so it was inclined 30 degrees to be used on their isometric drawings of their products.

Verifone was founded by William "Bill" Melton and incorporated in Hawaii in 1981, and named itself after its first product, the name standing for **Verif**ication teleph**one**. VeriFone is the transaction automation company that has made credit authorization terminals ubiquitous on retail merchant counters throughout the U.S.

Since the late 1980s, Verifone has held more than 60 percent of the U.S. market, and during the 1990s the company captured more than half of the international market for such systems. In 1996, the company placed its five millionth system. Domestic and international sales of POS (Point of Sales) systems continue to form the majority of Verifone's annual sales, which hit $387 million in 1995 and were expected to top $500 million in subsequent years.

The sudden growth of the Internet, and especially the World Wide Web in the mid-1990s created a demand for secure online financial transaction applications. Verifone has taken the lead in designing applications conforming to the Secure Electronic Transaction (SET) standards developed by Visa Inc. and MasterCard. With the $28 million 1995 acquisition of Enterprise Integration Technologies, the company that developed the Secure HyperText Transfer Protocol (SHTTP), and a $4 million equity investment in CyberCash, Inc., led by Verifone founder William Melton. With 1996 partnership agreements with Internet browser leaders Netscape, Oracle Corporation, and Microsoft, Verifone has rolled out a suite of software products targeted at consumers, merchants, and financial institutions allowing secure purchases and other transactions online. In 1997, Hewlett-Packard acquired Verifone in a $1.18 billion stock-swap deal. Four years later Verifone, was sold to Gores Technology Group in May 2001. In 2002 Verifone was recapitalized by GTCR Golder Rauner, LLC. In 2005, Verifone was listed as public company on New York Stock Exchange (NYSE: PAY). April 2018, CNBC's Kate Rogers reports on Verifone to be acquired by a group led by private equity firm Francisco Partners for $3.4 billion in an all-cash deal.

Source: Wikipedia

Sample of the VeriFone logo with the Cap-F which was changed
to the lower case " f " on 9 April 2018 and the
"Ribbon" graphic was removed. (Illustration by the author).

Verifone®

Current Registered Trademark modernized for today's branding.
It also fits better imprinted on their various hardware devices.

Chapter 2

Background on Studio 94
Logos and Trademark Samples,
Questions asked logo/trademark clients
and Quick Start Reference Guides
for USPTO and WIPO Madrid.

A sampling of Studio 94's Customers:

Apparel & Fashion (Logos, name tags and advertising)

Asian Products (Patent drawings & logos)

Aircraft Safety Equipment (Patent drawings, engineering & passing FAA inspection)

American Craft Products (Advertising)

Automobile Dealerships & Rental (Brochures & advertising)

Building Trade (Technical illustrations)

Business Stationary (Design & printing)

Election Flyers (Design & printing)

Food Packaging (Patent drawings & logos)

Footwear & Sandals (Logos/trademarks & advertising)

*Girl Scouts of Hawaii** (Graphics & brochures)

*Hawaiian Humane Society** (Logos & brochures)

Hawaiian Koa Wood Products (Logos, product tags & advertising)

Hawaiian Tee Shirts (Designs)

Independent Inventors & Entrepreneurs (Patent/trademark drawings, start-up graphics)

Intellectual Property Attorneys & Agents (Patent & trademark drawings)

Kapalua Shops, Kapalua, Maui (Photography, professional models & brochures)

Lanai things and products (Illustrations, catalogs & advertising)

Medical & Implant Devices (Patent drawings)

*Police Youth Programs** (Flyers & brochures)

Restaurants, some with Trade Dress (Advertising, menus and architect drawings)

Real Estate Development (Finalize logos/trademarks & advertising)

Sea Rescue Equipment (Patent drawings)

Surf & Boogie Boards (Patent drawings, logos/trademarks & advertising)

Tech Communication Equipment (Patent & technical illustrations)

Travel & Tourist (Brochures & advertising)

U.S. Navy Shipyard, Pearl Harbor (Patent drawings)

*Note: * - Pro Bono Work*

Original Corporate Logo   Current Logo

Studio 94 background

January, 1974 applied for the business name of Studio 94 as a partnership in the state of Hawaii, received State certificate, legal and tax papers on March 6, 1974.
Paid Hawaii State and IRS taxes under the name of Studio 94 from 1974 through 1978.

June 6, 1978 converted partnership into a corporation named
Studio 94 Designing Woman Ltd., dba Studio 94.
Paid Hawaii State and IRS taxes under the name of Studio 94 Designing Woman Ltd. from 1978 through 1994.

Sold the business in August of 1994 to one of our employees, but kept the name Studio 94, moved back to Ohio where we operated Studio 94 out of two offices in our house. Here we did graphic design, patent and trademark drawings under the name Studio 94. Paid business taxes under name STUDIO 94 as a soul proprietorship from 1995 through 2001.

Changed STUDIO 94 to STUDIO 94 Publishing in 2001 as soul proprietorship, writing, illustrating, publishing and paying taxes from 2001 through the present time.

First book (Pulled from Publishing) 2001

Title: PREPARING TRADEMARK DRAWINGS & SPECIMENS
Sub-title: for Electronic Transmission to the United States Patent and Trademark Office
Author/Illustrator: Murray H. Henderson
Copyright: 2002 Studio 94 Publishing
Remarks: Pulled book from publishing do to many graphic software changes at that time these changes would have caused my main theme of my book to be incorrect.

Second book, published in 2011

Title: ILLUSTRATED PATENT DRAWING STANDARDS
Sub-title: Illustrated Patent Drawing Standards of the United States Patent and Trademark Office (USPTO) and the Patent Cooperation Treaty (PCT) for International Applications
ISBN: 978-0-9828270-3-1
Library of Congress Control Number: 2010916633
Copyright: 2011
Author/Illustrator: Murray H. Henderson
Editor: Meredith C. Prock
Book Distributer: INGRAM

Third book, published in 2016

Title: PATENT DRAWING RULES
Sub-title: United States Patent and Trademark Office and the World Intellectual
  Property Organization Domestic, PCT and Hague Agreement Rules
ISBN: 978-0-9828270-2-4
Copyright: 2016
Author/Illustrator: Murray H. Henderson
Editor: Meredith C. Prock
Book Distributer: INGRAM

Forth book, published in 2020

Title: Guide for Logo and TRADEMARK DRAWINGS
Sub-title: Graphic requirements of the USPTO and WIPO's Madrid International
  Trademark System
ISBN: 978-0-9828270-4-8
Copyright: 2020
Author/Illustrator: Murray H. Henderson
Editor: Anne E. Bauswein
Book Distributer: INGRAM

Books in production:
Guide for Design PATENT DRAWINGS
Guide for Nonprovisional PATENT DRAWINGS

TMEP § 807.05(c) Requirements for Digitized Images

1 - **Special Form Drawing** .jpg format.
2 - Cropped little or no white space
3 - Application Form box (electronic/paper)

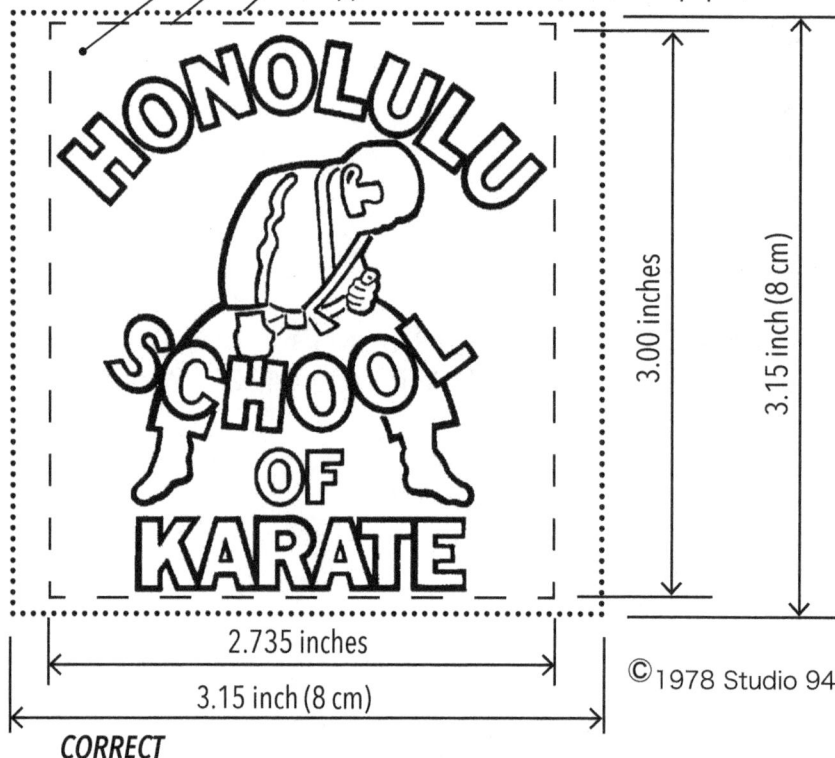

3.00 inches

3.15 inch (8 cm)

2.735 inches

3.15 inch (8 cm)

©1978 Studio 94

CORRECT

TMEP § 807 Drawing:
§ 807.05(c) Requirements for Digitized Images

Mark images should have little or no white space appearing around the design of the mark. . . .

Failure to do this may cause the mark to appear very small in the USPTO's automated records, such that it may be difficult to recognize all words or design features of the mark. . . .

If the mark is not clear, the examining attorney must require a new **drawing** that meets the requirements of 37 C.F.R. §§2.52 and 2.54

INCORRECT

Illustration showing correct and incorrect way of cropping a mark image for submittal to the USPTO's Trademark Electronic Application System (TEAS).

Sample work of Studio 94 designs, logos and trademarks

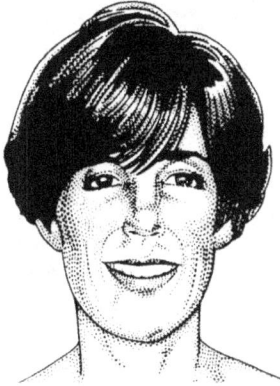

Evelyn Ryder Henderson
Studio 94/Designing Woman, Ltd.
Owner, Graphic Designer

Trademark Design for
The WOW Company Inc., Honolulu, Hawaii
(Original Mark in color)

Trademark for the
Hawaii Newspaper Agency, Honolulu, Hawaii
(Original Mark in color, 1974)

Trademark Design for Scott Hawaii
Original Mark in color, 1978

Design in color for
Crazy Shirts Hawaii

Logo/Trademark designs by Studio 94 with copyright assigned to their business entities.

Illustrations By
Evelyn Ryder Henderson

Teeshirt Design

ON STAGE Nov. 30 thru Dec. 24, 1977

THE TRIAL OF
LILIUOKALANI
by Maurice Zimm

Hawaii Performing Arts Company
MANOA VALLEY THEATRE, 2833 E. MANOA ROAD

Program Cover

DENDROBIUM
HAWAII'S LIVELIEST ORCHID

When your flowers are Dendrobiums, you know someone thinks you are special.

Trademark Design in color

Graphic Designs by Evelyn Ryder Henderson

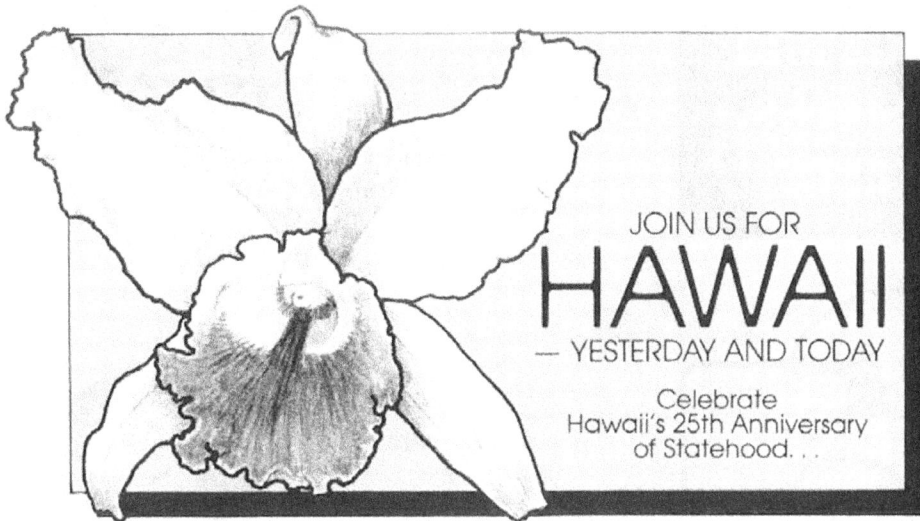

JOIN US FOR
HAWAII
— YESTERDAY AND TODAY

Celebrate
Hawaii's 25th Anniversary
of Statehood...

Design for Hawaii State

LAULIMA JAMBOREE
1992
GIRL SCOUT COUNCIL OF HAWAII

Pro bono Design for Girl Scouts

Aloha Fashion Week Graphic

Trademarks Logos and Business Brands

Rodney K.T. Kam
Studio 94
Graphic Designer
Illustrator

**Logo Design for the
Aloha Week Sponsors**

NORIKO'S
H A W A I I

Logo for a Honolulu jewelry business

Logo Design for the
Hawaii Humane Society's
Spay-Neuter Program

© 1986

TURTLES
H A W A I I

Logo for an Animal Protection Group

Logo/Trademark designs by Studio 94 with copyright assigned to their business entities.

Murray H. Henderson
Studio 94 Owner
Technical Illustrator
and Author

**Trademarks
Logos and
Business
Brands**

Design for Crazy Shirts
Hawaii 1975
Primo Hawaiian Beer®
is a Trademark of the
Joseph Schlitz
Brewing Co.

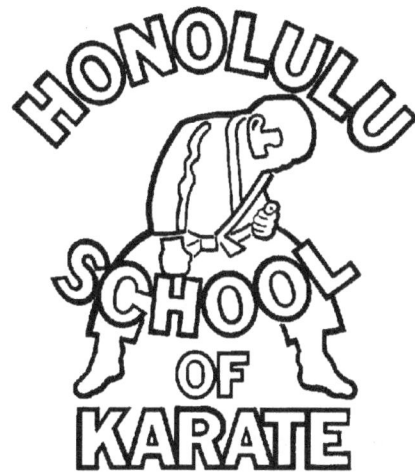

PRIMO
HAWAIIAN BEER
ISLAND BREWED

*Leather
Together*

Hand Made in HAWAII

Logo Design for leather products
used for apparel identification

HONOLULU
SCHOOL
OF
KARATE

LOGO/ Tee-Shirt Design
© 1975 Studio 94

PESCO
B-W
PRODUCTS
BORG-WARNER

Pesco Products
Division
of the Borg-Warner
Corporation,
Logo-Trademark
reworked for
better reproduction

TRUST IN GOD
LIBERTY
SHE WILL PROVIDE

Design for Crazy Shirts Hawaii
1976

Logo/Trademark designs by Studio 94 with copyright assigned to their business entities.

Questions Studio 94 asked logo/trademark clients

- 1 - Have you done a business name or trademark search?
- 2 - Where are you going to display your logo/trademark?
- 3 - Do you want the Mark to describe your business?
- 4 - Do you want your Mark to identify a product?
- 5 - Will your Mark be in color?
- 6 - If you use color, does it have meaning?
- 7 - How much information do you want on your Mark?
- 8 - If you specify a font, do you need permission to use it?
- 9 - Use of foreign words: Do you really know their meaning?
- 10 - Certain symbolic numbers are bad luck in some countries.

(1) Have you done a business name or trademark search?

Amazingly only about 50% of clients did this. At the present it is much easier to do a search on your state's business database, the USPTO TESS Search, WIPO's Madrid Global Brand Database.

(2) Where are you going to display your logo/trademark?

Where a Logo/Trademark is displayed tells the graphic designer how to space font type and how to make a graphic image recognizable. For example, artists through all generations have the tendency to space letters very close together; that's ok if you are viewing the logo/mark up close but at a distance it becomes illegible.
The shape of the logo/mark also needs to be matched to where you will place it on your product. Example: The older Verifone mark with the ribbon made the height of the mark too high and to able to fit in small areas on Point of Sales terminals, whereas their new mark fits well with all uses: business cards, stationery, web-site and their various products.

Current Verifone Registered mark

Old Verifone "Ribbon" Logo

(3) Do you want the Mark to describe your business?

Do you want your logo/mark to illustrate what your business is and does?
Do you anticipate being a "one product or service company" or do you anticipate many products?
If yes, then the mark should illustrate good communication so people can find you.

(4) Do you want your Mark to identify a product?

If you want to identify a particular product then it will be in the Branding category.
If so, do you anticipate the product evolving or having spin-offs or will it stay as first produced.

(5) Do you want your logo/mark in color(s)?

If yes, some things to consider:
a) Don't use the same color as a competitor;

b) Use a color that is in contrast to what it is displayed on, for example a darker value color on a fleet of white trucks.

c) Don't use a light value color such as yellow on a white background. There are a lot of registered marks that have claimed yellow as a color and when they had their mark displayed on their new web-site and it was too hard to see, so the web-site designer changed the yellow to an orange color. If I had a dollar for every time I have seen this, and of course, the specimen will not match the applicant's mark.

d) Are you anticipating a variety of products that, to easily recognize them, you may want to color code the logo/marks?

e) Do you want us to come up with some color suggestions?

(6) If you use color does it have meaning?

Some logo/marks have a direct relationship to colors for example, we did a lot of pro bono work for the Girl Scouts of America and they had a particular green color, the U.S. Air Force's blue, etc.

(7) How much information do you want on your mark?

I was always surprised by future clients who did not want their address or telephone numbers in connection to their logo/marks, saying "everyone knows who we are and where we are." This was especially true when we made up media ads for them.
A lot of marks today have a "tag-line" usually on the bottom listing their web-site.

(8) If you want a particular font do you have permission to use it?

Type fonts have a mixed history of how they are protected, who owns them and do you have to pay for using them. The first design patent issued in the United States of America was for a type font and amazingly it did not include drawings!
Some fonts only have their name protected, others have a design patent and there are other licensing protections.

An example, Bruce Hopper Designs in 1978 created the Kapalua Butterfly Logo and with the use of the logo he altered, with permission, the Palatino font. It was called then "Kapalua Palatino." I had the Kapalua Shops as a client doing some advertising and producing their 4-panel 4 x 9 Kapalua Shops catalog. Working on their projects I had to get the specifications on how to use the altered font, the logo color and where to position the font text in relation to the logo. The Kapalua Resorts then consisted of the Beach Hotel, Condos, Shops and the Golf Course. (The golf course was originally a pineapple ranch. That's why Bruce chose the pineapple shape for the butterfly logo's body.)

The Kapalua Shops

100 Bay drive • Kapalua, Maui, Hawaii 96761

(9) Use of foreign words: Do you really know their meaning?

One of my clients invented an aqua-lung breathing device and gave it "a cute foreign slang name" that his wife brought back from a recent European trip. He then used that name on his new product. As soon as he had working models, he went on a promotional tour of the U.S.A. and it was well received. Then he took his tour to Europe and when he announced the product name, the audience started laughing.
It seems his "cute little foreign word" translated into "Ladies of the Evening" in Europe.

(10) Certain symbolic numbers are bad luck in some countries.

Certain numbers or number of parts used in a logo can be detrimental. For example, in Japan the number four is considered bad luck, four in Japanese is "shi" which is also the word for death.

I have designed logos for Japanese clients and they would always remind me not to use four elements in their logos. I also knew the meaning of "shi" because I was in Judo for 6 years, where I learned counting in Japanese, not death.

Trademark "Special Form Drawing" Quick Reference Guides
Code numbers, specifications and sizing for application trademarks

CODE:	DESCRIPTION:
1	Typed drawings prior to November 2, 2003
2	Special Form Drawing: Design Only
3	Special Form Drawing: Design plus Words/Numbers
4	Standard Character Drawings
5	Special Form Drawing: Stylized Letters and Numerals
6	Non-Visual Marks

807.05(C) REQUIREMENTS FOR DIGITIZED IMAGES

The mark image must be in .jpg format, and should be scanned at no less than 300 dots per inch and no more than 350 dots per inch, to produce the highest quality image. All lines must be clean, sharp, and solid, must not be fine or crowded, and must produce a high-quality image. 37 C.F.R §2.53(c). It is recommended that mark images have a length of no less than 250 pixels and no more than 944 pixels, and a width of no less than 250 pixels and no more than 944 pixels.

Mark images should have little or no white space appearing around the design of the mark. If scanning from a paper image of the mark, it may be necessary to cut out the mark and scan it with little or no surrounding white space. **Failure to do this may cause the mark to appear very small** in the USPTO's automated records, such that it may be difficult to recognize all words or design features of the mark. To ensure that there is a clear image of the mark in the automated records of the USPTO, examining attorneys and LIEs should view the mark on the Publication Review program available on the USPTO's internal computer network. If the mark is not clear, the examining attorney must require a new drawing that meets the requirements of 37 C.F.R. §§2.52–2.54.

When color is not claimed as a feature of the mark, the image must be depicted only in black and white. **When scanning an image, the applicant should confirm that the settings on the scanner are set to create a black-and-white image file, not a color image file.**

Mark images may not include **extraneous matter** such as the symbols TM or SM, or the registration notice ®. The image should be limited to the mark. See TMEP §807.02.

The drawing may not include extraneous matter such as the letters "TM," "SM," the copyright notice ©, or the federal registration notice ®.
See TMEP §§906–906.04 regarding use of the federal registration notice.

See TMEP §807.14(a) regarding requirements for removal of matter from the drawing.

USPTO requirements for file attachments to TEAS forms

We accept image files in PDF or JPG format. **Drawing files (mark images) must be submitted in JPG format**, see requirements for drawing files for more information. You may submit all other image files (specimens, evidence, etc.) in either format.

JPG requirements:

- JPG files must be 5MB or smaller.
- The filename can be up to 256 characters long, including the ".jpg" extension.

You are encouraged to use the shortest filename possible. Remember to save images created on a Macintosh using Adobe Photoshop or Illustrator with the .jpg extensions.

PDF requirements:

Size
- All files must be 30MB or smaller
- All files must be saved at 300 DPI
- Page size within the files must be set to 14 x 14 inches or smaller
  If any page within the entire PDF file exceeds this size limitation, the entire PDF file will be blocked from upload.

Format
- Use a valid PDF format. It is NOT sufficient that the file simply be named using a PDF extension (.pdf), because that does not by itself create a valid PDF file.
- Use one of the formats below for images within the PDF file.
  GIF, BMP, TIFF, JPG or PNG
- Use one of the fonts below.
  Courier (Regular, Bold, Italic, or Bold Italic), Times (Roman, Bold, Italic, or Bold Italic), Helvetica (Regular, Bold, Italic, or Bold Italic), Symbol, Zapf Dingbats.

NOTE: Fonts not listed above must be embedded within the PDF document.
- Fonts should be set to "subset."

Filename
- Can use upper or lower case letters or numbers, periods (.), underscores (_), or hyphens (-)
- No spaces
  Spaces are permitted in the file path, (the file's location on your computer), but never in the name of the file itself.
- Must end in .pdf
- Can be up to 256 characters long (including the .pdf portion.
  Please use the shortest name possible.

USPTO requirements for trademark file attachments to TEAS forms

Do not include

- **Security settings**
  For example, self-sign security, user passwords, and/or permissions, or any other security settings that would prevent us from opening, viewing, or printing the file. All security settings must be deactivated (e.g., encryption, master passwords, and/or permissions).

- **Embedded scripts and/or executables**
  For example, interactive actions or form data importation scripts

- **Worms, viruses or other malicious content**
  Files with malicious content will be deleted.

- **Active hypertext links, or any internal/external links**
  While you may textually reference a URL as a disabled link, it cannot be presented as an actual hyperlink.

- **Embedded Objects**
  - **Multimedia**
    For example, sound, video, animations, slide shows
  - **3-dimensional models**
  - **Multi-page objects**
    For example, Excel spreadsheets
    While the overall PDF file would upload, the other internal object will be "stripped" out of the file, and will not be viewable.

Other requirements

- **All files must contain only a single layer.**
  Documents with multiple layers must be flattened prior to submission, to convert all overlapping areas in a stack of transparent objects into a collection of opaque objects.
  Any invisible layers will be lost when processed by the USPTO.

- **Use Adobe version 1.3 or newer.**
  NOTE: If you have Adobe Acrobat Professional 6.0, for instructions on resizing PDF pages or reducing the DPI, click here; otherwise, please forward the PDF file to TEAS@uspto.gov, for resizing/reduction within ONE (1) business day. Sending a file to the TEAS mailbox is NOT considered an actual "filing" for any deadline purposes.

7

THE MARK

(a) Place the reproduction of the mark, as it appears in the basic application or basic registration, in the square below.

(b) Where the reproduction in item (a) is in black and white and color is claimed in item 8, place a color reproduction of the mark in the square below.

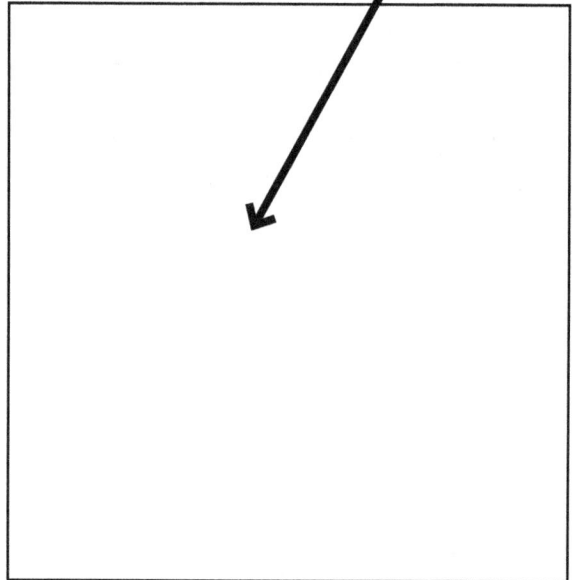

Pixel dimensions of no less than 250 or more than 944 (Example here: 855 x 851)

Image Width x Height

No less than 300 ppi & No more than 350 ppi (Example here 300 ppi)

Reference Material:
USPTO TESS Search
S/N: 76179959
Filling Date: Dec 12, 2000
Attorney: Robert J. Herberger

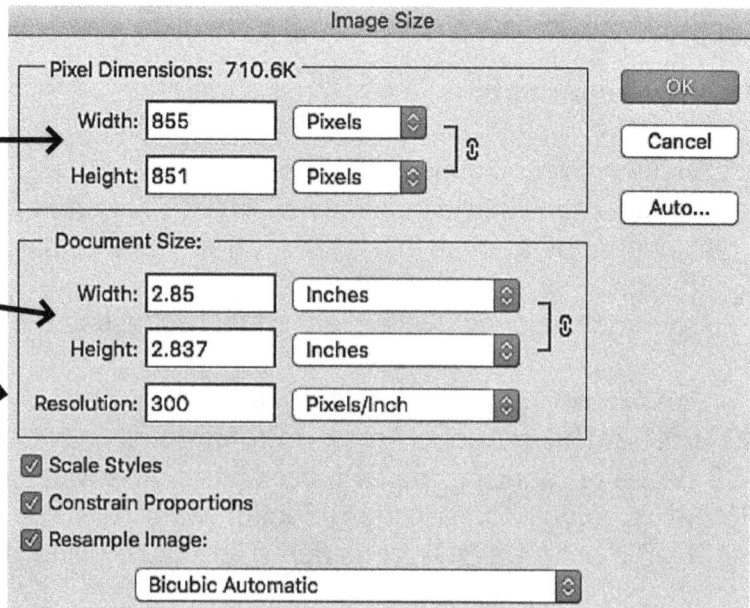

Studio 94 Scanning Tips for Patent and/or Trademark drawings

Scan Mode:	Flatbed
Kind:	[A] Text
Resolution:	600 dpi
	☑ Use Custom Size
Size:	8.34 9.86 inches
Rotation Angle:	0°
Auto Selection:	Off
Scan To:	Pictures
Name:	Scan
Format:	TIFF
	☐ Combine into single document

Three image scan formats:

a) Text* (1-bit monochrome)

b) Black & White (256 Grays)

c) Color (Millions)

* Where some make mistakes by scanning a line drawing in b) black & white which is a grayscale instead of a) Text which is for text or line drawings.

Save as Format:
Save as TIFF in 600 ppi or 1200 ppi if your files do not get too large

Image editing software (App):
Resize image to fit USPTO and/or WIPO Rules
Save As ...:
.jpg for Hague Design or Madrid Trademarks (300 ppi)
.pdf for above supporting documents.
.pdf for USPTO utility or design line drawing patents.
.tif for USPTO utility or design grayscale or color drawings. (600 or 1200 ppi)
Use file naming rules per USPTO and/or WIPO

AUTHOR'S COMMENTS
I realize that you may have a different scanning App, but I have observed the problem of applicants scanning in grayscale thinking it was line because the scanning App was too confusing.

Chapter 3

USPTO · TMEP Trademark Drawing Requirements
(The selected rules)

TMEP - Chapter 0800 Application Requirements

TMEP - Chapter 0900 Use in Commerce

TMEP - Chapter 1300 Service, Collective and
       Certification Marks

TMEP - Chapter 1400 Classification of Marks

TMEP - Chapter 1900 Madrid Protocol

INTRODUCTION TO CHAPTER 3
The USPTO and WIPO Madrid Trademark rules in this book
Chapter 3 covers the TMEP chapters 800, 900, 1300, 1400 and 1900

I have chosen only the trademark and specimen parts of the rules that pertain
to trademark drawings, reproduction and their digital files.
Specimens: Information on size, file types allowed and what may cause problems.
Digital files: On file types allowed, image minimum and maximum file size.

The USPTO & WIPO Rules are taken from their manuals and web-sites as of January
2020. The only changes I made to the rules was to highlight areas of attention for the
reader by the use of **bold type** or by "boxing in" special areas that need attention.

I have included information on "Standard Character Drawings" even though they aren't
a "Special Form Drawing," because applicants are always coming up with schemes to
manipulate type and call it a Standard Character Drawing, ways such as:

- Linking words or letters as a ligature;

- Using only a specific font, or

- Altering a font's letters and/or numbers in any way.

I know you can come up with samples but this does not make it right!
Anything you do other to type out your standard character font, in the fonts they
specify and only using the characters listed should fail.

The way we worked with Intellectual Property Attorneys
On trademarks, if Studio 94 created the mark and it was in color we gave the attorney
a complete color description. If the color described must be exact, generally the colors
were described as a PMS (Pantone Matching System), we made that clear; if it was not
that important then the colors were described generically as; red, blue, green, etc.

My opinion
I liked the old Madrid form MM2 where, if you had a mark that contains color, you were
required to place your mark in both boxes on page 3 of form MM2, box (a) as black
and white copy and in box (b) a color copy of your mark. I understand the reason at
that time, because the older Trademark Gazettes were printed in black and white.

I liked the "two-box application" from the standpoint that in the real world, no matter if
you have a color mark, there are times when your mark will be printed in mono-chrome.
Examples; on a fax sent out (yes, some reasons to use it), printed on newspapers that
are printed in black & white, printed on theatre programs and on various charity
publications, with each only printing in one color.

The trademark examples in this book are mostly in color, but this book is printed
in black and white.

TRADEMARK MANUAL OF EXAMINING PROCEDURE (TMEP)
UNITED STATES PATENT AND TRADEMARK OFFICE

October 2018

Foreword

*The **Trademark Manual of Examining Procedure*** (TMEP) may be downloaded free of charge from the United States Patent and Trademark Office (USPTO) website at http://www.uspto.gov/trademark/guides-and-manuals/tmep-archives.

The Manual is published to provide trademark examining attorneys in the USPTO, trademark applicants, and attorneys and representatives for trademark applicants with a reference work on the practices and procedures relative to prosecution of applications to register marks in the USPTO. The Manual contains guidelines for Examining Attorneys and materials in the nature of information and interpretation, and outlines the procedures which Examining Attorneys are required or authorized to follow in the examination of trademark applications.

Trademark Examining Attorneys will be governed by the applicable statutes, the Trademark Rules of Practice, decisions, and Orders and Notices issued by the Under Secretary of Commerce for Intellectual Property and Director of the United States Patent and Trademark Office, Commissioners, or Deputy Commissioners. Policies stated in this revision supersede any previous policies stated in prior editions, examination guides, or any other statement of Office policy, to the extent that there is any conflict.

Suggestions for improving the form and content of the Manual are always welcome. They should be e-mailed to tmtmep@uspto.gov, or addressed to:

Commissioner for Trademarks

Attention: Editor, *Trademark Manual of Examining Procedure*
P.O. Box 1451
Alexandria, Virginia
22313-1451
Catherine P. Cain, Editor

Mary Boney Denison
Commissioner for Trademarks

United States Patent & Trademark Office

TRADEMARK MANUAL OF EXAMINING PROCEDURE (TMEP)

October 2018

CONTENTS

AUTHOR'S COMMENTS
The subjects in bold type are in reference to
"Special Form Drawings" and/or the Applicants' "Specimens"

TMEP Chapter 0800

Application Requirements
(Drawing Requirements)

806.01(a) Use in Commerce - §1(a)

Under 15 U.S.C. §1051(a) and 37 C.F.R. §2.34(a)(1), to establish a basis under §1(a) of the Trademark Act, the applicant must:

(1) Submit a verified statement that the mark is in use in commerce. 15 U.S.C. §1051(a)(3)(C); 37 C.F.R. §§2.2(k)(1), 2.34(a)(1)(i). If this verified statement is not filed with the initial application, the verified statement must also allege that the mark was in use in commerce as of the application filing date (37 C.F.R. §§2.2(k)(1), 2.34(a)(1)(i));

(2) Specify the date of the applicant's first use of the mark anywhere on or in connection with the goods or services (37 C.F.R. §2.2(k)(1), 2.34(a)(1)(ii); TMEP §903.01);

(3) Specify the date of the applicant's first use of the mark in commerce (37 C.F.R. §§2.2(k)(1), 2.34(a)(1)(iii); TMEP §903.02); and

(4) Submit one specimen for each class, showing how the applicant uses the mark in commerce (37 C.F.R. §§2.34(a)(1)(iv), 2.56; TMEP §§904–904.07(b)).
The Trademark Act defines "commerce" as commerce which may lawfully be regulated by Congress, and "use in commerce" as the bona fide use of a mark in the ordinary course of trade. 15 U.S.C. §1127; see TMEP §§901–901.04.

An applicant may claim both use in commerce under §1(a) of the Act and intent-to-use under §1(b) of the Act as a filing basis in the same application, but may not assert both §1(a) and §1(b) for the identical goods or services in the same application. 37 C.F.R. §2.34(b); TMEP §806.02(b).

An applicant may not claim a §1(a) basis unless the mark was in use in commerce on or in connection with all the goods or services covered by the §1(a) basis as of the application filing date.   See 37 C.F.R. §§2.2(k)(1), 2.34(a)(1)(i); cf. E.I. du Pont de Nemours & Co. v. Sunlyra Int'l, Inc., 35 USPQ2d 1787, 1791 (TTAB 1995).

If the applicant claims use in commerce in addition to another filing basis, but does not specify which goods or services are covered by which basis, the USPTO may defer examination of the specimen(s) until the applicant identifies the goods or services for which use is claimed.   TMEP §806.02(c).

See TMEP §§1303.01(a)(i)-(a)(i)(C), 1304.02(a)(i)-(a)(i)(C), and 1306.02(a)(i)-(a)(i)(B) for the requirements for a §1(a) basis for collective and certification mark applications.

807 Drawing

The drawing shows the mark sought to be registered. 37 C.F.R. §2.52. An applicant **must submit a clear drawing** with the original application to receive a filing date in any application for registration of a mark, except in applications for registration of sound, scent, and other non-visual marks.   See 37 C.F.R. §§2.21(a)(3), 2.52(e). See also TMEP §807.09 regarding drawings in applications for registration of non-visual marks. Submitting a specimen showing how the mark is or may be used (e.g., the overall packaging, a photograph of the goods, or an advertisement) does not satisfy the requirement for a clear drawing of the mark.   See TMEP §202.01.

The drawing is used to reproduce the mark in the Trademark Official Gazette and on the registration certificate.

The main purpose of the drawing is to provide notice of the nature of the mark sought to be registered. The drawing of a mark is promptly entered into the automated records of the USPTO and is available to the public through the Trademark Electronic Search System ("TESS") and the Trademark Status and Document Retrieval ("TSDR") database on the USPTO website at http://tsdr.uspto.gov/. Timely public notification of the filing of applications is important, because granting a filing date to an application potentially establishes a date of constructive use of the mark (see TMEP §201.02). Therefore, an application under §1 or §44 must include a clear drawing of the mark to receive a filing date. 37 C.F.R. §2.21(a)(3); TMEP §202.01.

Examining attorneys must require applicants to comply promptly with the drawing rules. Requests to defer drawing corrections until the application is approved for publication or registration must be denied.

There are two forms of drawings: "special form drawings" and "standard character drawings." See 37 C.F.R. §§2.52(a), (b). See also TMEP §§807.03–807.03(i) for information about standard character drawings, and TMEP §§807.04–807.04(b) for information about special form drawings. (Note: "Typed" drawings are acceptable for applications filed before November 2, 2003.   See TMEP §807.03(i).)

For special form marks, generally, the most appropriate drawing of the mark shows an illustrated rendering of the mark. However, a photograph may also be acceptable if it accurately depicts the mark and does not show additional matter that is not part of the mark. For example, a photograph of trade dress is not acceptable if it includes unnecessary background information or informational matter such as net weight or contents.

Drawings consisting of either illustrated renderings or photographs of the mark are both subject to the same drawing requirements and must fairly represent the mark.

The mark in the drawing must agree with the mark as used on the specimen

in an application under §1 of the Trademark Act, 15 U.S.C. §1051; as applied for or registered in a foreign country in an application under §44, 15 U.S.C. §1126; or as it appears in the international registration in an application under §66(a), 15 U.S.C. §1141f(a). 37 C.F.R. §2.51(a)–(d); TMEP §§807.12–807.12(c), 1011.01.

In a TEAS application, the drawing must be submitted electronically through TEAS, and must meet the requirements of 37 C.F.R. §§2.52 and 2.53 (see TMEP §§807.05–807.05(c)). In a paper application, the drawing must be submitted on paper and must meet the requirements of 37 C.F.R. §§2.52 and 2.54 (see TMEP §§807.06–807.06(c)).

AUTHOR'S COMMENTS

In my experience, the mark not "agreeing" with the specimen shows up quite frequently due to multiple people getting involved with the specimens; type, colors, printing, web-sites, packaging, etc.

This is why graphic design firms work with legal departments and coordinate on how the trademark must be used. They produce an instruction manual that tells users where and how to place the mark; which size, color (generally PMS specified). The instructions generally have an assortment of various size trademarks printed to be used as clip-art along with instructions on which size to be used where. At the current time the instruction manuals are digital.

This is why the good design firms get the big dollars, because there is a lot more to it than the artwork!

A mark may appear as a Standard Character mark or as a Special Form mark. A Standard Character mark is the most flexible of all mark depictions. It grants protection to the wording itself, without regard to the font, style, size, or color. Although the mark looks like plain typed wording when registered, a Standard Character mark means that you can change how you display the wording over the life of the trademark. Not bad for a simple looking mark, right?
Source: USPTO Instruction video

807.01   Drawing Must Show Only One Mark

An application must be limited to only one mark. 15 U.S.C. §1051(a)(1); 37 C.F.R. §2.52. See In re Int'l Flavors & Fragrances Inc., 183 F.3d 1361, 1366, 51 USPQ2d 1513, 1516 (Fed. Cir. 1999)

Under 37 C.F.R. §2.21(a)(3), an applicant must submit **"a clear drawing of the mark"** to receive a filing date. An application that includes two or more drawings displaying materially different marks does not meet this requirement. Two marks are considered to be materially different if the substitution of one for the other would be a material alteration of the mark, within the meaning of 37 C.F.R. §2.72 (see TMEP §§807.14–807.14(f)).

Accordingly, if an applicant submits two or more drawing pages, the application is denied a filing date, because the applicant has not met the requirement for a clear drawing of the mark. See TMEP §202.01 for further information.   See also Humanoids Grp. v. Rogan, 375 F.3d 301, 307-309, 71 USPQ2d 1745, 1750-1751 (4th Cir. 2004). However, if an applicant submits a separate drawing page in a paper application showing a mark, and a different mark appears in the written application, the application will receive a filing date, and the drawing page will control for purposes of determining what the mark is. The USPTO will disregard the mark in the written application. In re L.G. Lavorazioni Grafite S.r.l., 61 USPQ2d 1063, 1064 (Dir USPTO 2001). Similarly, if an applicant enters a standard character mark, or attaches a digitized image of a mark, in the "Mark" field of a TEAS application, and a different mark appears in another field, the application will receive a filing date, and the mark entered in the "Mark" field will control for purposes of determining what the mark is.

The USPTO will not deny a filing date if the drawing shows spatially separate elements. If the applicant submits an application where the "drawing" is composed of multiple elements on a separate page, multiple elements on a single digitized image, or multiple elements in a separate area of the body of the application, the applicant has met the requirement of 37 C.F.R. §2.21(a)(3) for a clear drawing of the mark. The examining attorney must determine whether the matter presented for registration is a single mark projecting a unitary commercial impression. See TMEP §807.12(d) regarding "mutilation" or incomplete representation of the mark.

If the examining attorney determines that spatially separate elements constitute two or more different marks, the examining attorney must refuse registration under §§1 and 45 of the Trademark Act, 15 U.S.C. §§1051 and 1127, on the ground that the applicant seeks registration of more than one mark. This refusal may apply in any application, regardless of the filing basis.

807.01 Drawing must show only one mark continued

Under 37 C.F.R. §2.52(b)(2), even if registration is sought for a *three-dimensional mark,* the applicant must submit a drawing depicting a single rendition of the mark. See TMEP §807.10. If the applicant submits a drawing that depicts a three-dimensional mark in multiple renditions, the examining attorney will require a substitute drawing depicting the mark in a single rendition. If the applicant believes that its mark cannot be adequately depicted in a single rendition, the applicant may file a petition under 37 C.F.R. §2.146 requesting that the rule be waived. See TMEP Chapter 1700 regarding petitions.

If the mark is duplicated in some form on the drawing (e.g., a typed word and a stylized display of the same word), this is generally not considered to be two materially different marks, and deletion of one of the marks is permitted.

See TMEP §§1214–1214.04 regarding the refusal of registration of a mark with a "phantom" element on the ground that it includes more than one mark in a single application.

See also In re Upper Deck Co., 59 USPQ2d 1688, 1691 (TTAB 2001) (holding that a hologram used on trading cards in varying shapes, sizes, contents, and positions constitutes more than one "device" as contemplated by §45 of the Trademark Act).

807.02 Drawing Must Be Limited to Mark

The drawing allows the USPTO to properly code and index the mark for search purposes, indicates what the mark is, and provides a means for reproducing the mark in the Official Gazette and on the certificate of registration. Therefore, matter that appears on the specimen that is not part of the mark should not be placed on the drawing. Purely informational matter such as net weight, contents, or business addresses are generally not considered part of the mark.

> Quotation marks and hyphens should not be included in the mark on a drawing, unless they are a part of the mark. See TMEP §§807.12(a)(i)–807.14(a)(iii) and 807.14(c) regarding the role of punctuation in determining whether the mark on the drawing agrees with the mark on the specimen. **The drawing may not include extraneous matter such as the letters "TM," "SM," the copyright notice ©, or the federal registration notice ®. See TMEP §§906–906.04 regarding use of the federal registration notice.**
>
> See TMEP §807.14(a) regarding requirements for removal of matter from the drawing.

807.03   Standard Character Drawings

37 C.F.R. §2.52(a) Standard character (typed) drawing.

Applicants who seek to register words, letters, numbers, or any combination thereof without claim to any particular font style, size, or color must submit a standard character drawing that shows the mark in black on a white background. An applicant may submit a standard character drawing if:

• (1) The application includes a statement that the mark is in standard characters and

    no claim is made to any particular font style, size, or color;

• (2) The mark does not include a design element;

• (3) All letters and words in the mark are depicted in Latin characters;

• (4) All numerals in the mark are depicted in Roman or Arabic numerals; and

• (5) The mark includes only common punctuation or diacritical marks.

Effective November 2, 2003, Trademark Rule 2.52, 37 C.F.R. §2.52, was amended to replace the term "typed" drawing with "standard character" drawing. Applicants who seek to register a mark without any claim as to the manner of display must submit a standard character drawing that complies with the requirements of 37 C.F.R. §2.52(a).

807.03(a)   Requirements for Standard Character Drawings

A standard character drawing must show the mark in black on a white background. An applicant may submit a standard character drawing if:

• The mark does not include a design element;

• All letters and words in the mark are depicted in Latin characters;

• All numerals in the mark are depicted in Roman or Arabic numerals;

• The mark includes only common punctuation or diacritical marks; and

• No stylization of lettering and/or numbers is claimed in the mark.

37 C.F.R. §2.52(a).

> If the applicant files an application on paper that includes a standard character claim, the applicant may depict the mark in any font style; may use bold or italicized letters; and may use both uppercase and lowercase letters, all uppercase letters, or all lowercase letters, since no claim is made to any particular font style, size, or color. However, the USPTO will convert applicant's depiction of the mark to a standardized typeface for printing in the Official Gazette and on the registration certificate. If filing electronically via the Trademark Electronic Application System ("TEAS"), the applicant may neither depict the mark in any particular font style nor use bold or italicized letters. TEAS will automatically convert any wording typed into the standard-character field to a standardized typeface.

Superscripts, subscripts, exponents, or other characters that are not in the USPTO's standard character set (seeTMEP §807.03(b)) are not permitted in standard character drawings. In re AFG Indus. Inc., 17 USPQ2d 1162, 1163-64 (TTAB 1990) (holding that a special form drawing is required for a drawing featuring a raised numeral). The degree symbol is permitted.

Underlining is not permitted in a standard character drawing.

Standard Character Claim Required. An applicant who submits a standard character drawing must also submit the following standard character claim:

The mark consists of standard characters without claim to any particular font style, size, or color.

This statement will appear in the Official Gazette and on the certificate of registration.

807.04   Special Form Drawings

37 C.F.R. §2.52(b) (Extract) Special form drawing.

Applicants who seek to register a mark that includes a two or three-dimensional design; color; and/or words, letters, or numbers or the combination thereof in a particular font style or size must submit a special form drawing. The drawing should show the mark in black on a white background, unless the mark includes color.

807.04(a)   Characteristics of Special Form Drawings

A "special form drawing" is a drawing that presents a mark comprised, in whole or in part, of special characteristics such as elements of design or color, style(s) of lettering, or unusual form(s) of punctuation.

All special form drawings must be of a quality that will reproduce satisfactorily for scanning into the Trademark database. If the drawing is not of a quality that will reproduce satisfactorily for scanning and printing in the Official Gazette and on the certificate of registration, the examining attorney must require a new drawing. If there is any doubt as to whether the drawing is acceptable, the examining attorney should contact the Office of Trademark Quality Review.

Pasted material, taped material, and correction fluid are not acceptable because they do not reproduce satisfactorily.

See TMEP §807.18 concerning mark drawing codes.

A Special Form mark, on the other hand, is a mark that comprises special characteristics, like fonts or designs or colors. Special Form marks can be broken down into two categories: Stylized marks and Design marks. A Stylized mark is a mark in which the wording appears in a particular font. A Design mark can be a composite mark, in which you protect wording that is combined with a design. Or, it can be a mark comprised of design elements alone.

Remember, then, to submit a Special Form drawing when you want trademark protection for a particular design, stylization of wording, or combination of the two. If you want protection for wording alone, without regard to font, style, or color, the Standard Character format might be the one for you. **Source: USPTO Video**

807.05 Electronically Submitted Drawings

The drawing in a TEAS application must meet the requirements of 37 C.F.R. §§2.52–2.53.

The USPTO has waived the requirement of 37 C.F.R. §2.53(c) that drawings have a length and width of no less than 250 pixels and no more than 944 pixels. See 69 Fed. Reg. 59809 (Oct. 6, 2004). However, applicants are encouraged to continue to submit drawings with a length and width of no less than 250 pixels and no more than 944 pixels.

807.05(b) Special Form Drawings Submitted Electronically

If the mark is in special form, the applicant must attach a digitized image of the mark that meets the requirements of 37 C.F.R. §2.53(c) to the "Mark" field on the electronic application. See TMEP §807.05(c) regarding the requirements for digitized images.

807.05(C) REQUIREMENTS FOR DIGITIZED IMAGES

The mark image must be in .jpg format, and should be scanned at no less than 300 dots per inch and no more than 350 dots per inch, to produce the highest quality image. All lines must be clean, sharp, and solid, must not be fine or crowded, and must produce a high-quality image. 37 C.F.R §2.53(c). It is recommended that mark images have a length of no less than 250 pixels and no more than 944 pixels, and a width of no less than 250 pixels and no more than 944 pixels.

Mark images should have little or no white space appearing around the design of the mark. If scanning from a paper image of the mark, it may be necessary to cut out the mark and scan it with little or no surrounding white space. Failure to do this may cause the mark to appear very small in the USPTO's automated records, such that it may be difficult to recognize all words or design features of the mark. To ensure that there is a clear image of the mark in the automated records of the USPTO, examining attorneys and LIEs should view the mark on the Publication Review program available on the USPTO's internal computer network. If the mark is not clear, the examining attorney must require a new drawing that meets the requirements of 37 C.F.R. §§2.52–2.54.

When color is not claimed as a feature of the mark, the image must be depicted only in black and white. When scanning an image, the applicant should confirm that the settings on the scanner are set to create a black-and-white image file, not a color image file.

Mark images may not include extraneous matter such as the symbols TM or SM, or the registration notice ®. The image should be limited to the mark. See TMEP §807.02.

807.06 Paper Drawings

37 C.F.R. §2.52(d). Paper drawings. A paper drawing must meet the requirements of §2.54.

37 C.F.R. §2.54. Requirements for drawings submitted on paper.

The drawing must meet the requirements of §2.52. In addition, in a paper submission, the drawing should:

(a) Be on non-shiny white paper that is separate from the application;

(b) Be on paper that is 8 to 8.5 inches (20.3 to 21.6 cm.) wide and 11 to 11.69 inches (27.9 to 29.7 cm.) long. One of the shorter sides of the sheet should be regarded as its top edge. The image must be no larger than 3.15 inches (8 cm) high by 3.15 inches (8 cm) wide;

(c) Include the caption "DRAWING PAGE" at the top of the drawing beginning one inch (2.5 cm.) from the top edge; and

(d) Depict the mark in black ink, or in color if color is claimed as a feature of the mark.

(e) Drawings must be typed or made with a pen or by a process that will provide high definition when copied. A photo-lithographic, printer's proof copy, or other high quality reproduction of the mark may be used. All lines must be clean, sharp and solid, and must not be fine or crowded.

Paper drawings may be filed by mail or hand delivery. Drawings may not be submitted by facsimile transmission. 37 C.F.R. §2.195(d)(2).

The drawing must meet the requirements of 37 C.F.R. §§2.52 and 2.54.

```
Effective Date: February 15, 2020
USPTO rule makes electronic filing mandatory
for trademark submissions
```

807.07   Color in the Mark

37 C.F.R. §2.52(b)(1) Marks that include color.

If the mark includes color, the drawing must show the mark in color, and the applicant must name the color(s), describe where the color(s) appear on the mark, and submit a claim that the color(s) is a feature of the mark.

If the applicant wishes to register the mark in color, the applicant must submit a color drawing and meet the requirements of 37 C.F.R. §2.52(b)(1). See TMEP §§807.07(a)–807.07(g) regarding the requirements for color drawings. If the applicant does not claim color as a feature of the mark, the applicant must submit a black-and-white drawing.

Generally, if the applicant has not made a color claim, the description of the mark should not mention color(s), because reference to color in the description of a non-color mark creates a misleading impression.   TMEP §808.02. However, in some cases, it may be appropriate to submit a black-and-white drawing and a description of the mark that refers to black, white, and/or gray, if the applicant states that color is not claimed as a feature of the mark. This occurs where the black, white, and/or gray is used as a means to indicate areas that are not part of the mark, such as background or transparent areas; to depict a certain aspect of the mark that is not a feature of the mark, such as broken- or dotted-line outlining to show placement of the mark; to represent shading or stippling; or to depict depth or three-dimensional shape. See TMEP §§807.07(f)–807.07(f)(ii) regarding applications with black-and-white drawings and mark descriptions that refer to black, white, or gray with no corresponding color claim, TMEP §§807.07(d)–807.07(d)(iii) regarding color drawings that contain black, white, or gray, and TMEP §807.07(e) regarding black-and-white drawings and color claims.

See TMEP §§1202.05–1202.05(i) regarding the registration of marks that consist solely of one or more colors used on particular objects.

807.07(A)   REQUIREMENTS FOR COLOR DRAWINGS

For applications filed on or after November 2, 2003, the USPTO does not accept black-and-white drawings with a color claim, or drawings that show color by use of lining patterns. See 37 C.F.R. §2.52(b)(1).

If the mark includes color, the drawing must show the mark in color. In addition, the application must include: (1) a claim that the color(s) is/are a feature of the mark; and (2) a color location statement in the "Description of the Mark" field naming the color(s) and describing where the color(s) appear(s) on the mark. 37 C.F.R. §2.52(b)(1). A color drawing will not publish without both of these statements. See TMEP §807.07(a)(i) regarding the color claim, and TMEP §807.07(a)(ii) regarding the color location statement.

807.07(A)(II)   APPLICANT MUST SPECIFY THE LOCATION OF THE COLORS CLAIMED

> IIf an applicant submits a color drawing, in addition to claiming the color(s), the applicant must include a separate statement specifying where the color(s) appear(s) on the mark. 37 C.F.R. §2.52(b)(1). This statement is often referred to as a "color location statement." In a TEAS application, the color location statement should be set forth in the "Description of the Mark" field. A properly worded color location statement would read as follows:
>
> The mark consists of <specify the color(s) and literal or design element(s) on which the color(s) appear, e.g., a red bird sitting on a green leaf>.

If the color location statement is incorrect, incomplete, or inconsistent with the color(s) shown on the drawing, the color location statement must be corrected to conform to the color(s) depicted on the drawing. If the statement references changeable colors, the examining attorney must require an amended mark description that deletes the reference to the color in the mark varying or being changeable and restricts the description to only those colors shown on the drawing. See TMEP §807.01. However, if the record contains an accurate and properly worded color claim listing all the colors, and an informal description of where the colors appear, but one of the colors is omitted from the formal description of the colors in the mark, the examining attorney may enter an amendment of the color description that accurately reflects the location of all colors in the mark without prior approval by the applicant or the applicant's qualified practitioner.   See TMEP §707.02.

Example – A TEAS applicant includes a statement in the "Miscellaneous" field that refers to the mark as a blue, red, and yellow ball and includes an accurate and properly worded color claim listing all colors in the mark, but omits the color yellow from the description of the mark. The examining attorney may enter an amendment of the description to accurately reflect all colors in the mark.

The color location statement must include the generic name of the color claimed. The statement may also include a reference to a commercial color identification system. The USPTO does not endorse or recommend any one commercial color identification system.

It is usually not necessary to indicate shades of a color, but the examining attorney has the discretion to require that the applicant indicate shades of a color, if necessary to accurately describe the mark.

See TMEP §1202.05(e) for additional information regarding the requirement for a written explanation of a mark consisting solely of color.

807.07(a)(i) Color Must Be Claimed as a Feature of the Mark

If an applicant submits a color drawing, or a description of the mark that indicates the use of color on the mark, the applicant must claim color as a feature of the mark. 37 C.F.R. §2.52(b)(1). If the color claim is incorrect, incomplete, or inconsistent with the color(s) shown on the drawing, the color claim must be corrected to conform to the color(s) depicted on the drawing. If the color claim or mark description references changeable colors, the examining attorney must require an amended mark description that deletes the reference to the color in the mark varying or being changeable and restricts the description to only those colors shown on the drawing. See TMEP §807.01. Alternatively, the applicant may amend to a black-and-white drawing, if the amendment would not constitute a material alteration. A properly worded color claim would read as follows:

The color(s) *<name the color(s)>* is/are claimed as a feature of the mark.

The color claim must include the generic name of the color(s) claimed. It is usually not necessary to indicate shades of a color, but the examining attorney has the discretion to require that the applicant do so, if necessary to accurately describe the mark. The color claim may also include a reference to a commercial color identification system. The USPTO does not endorse or recommend any one commercial color identification system.

In an application filed on or after November 2, 2003, an applicant cannot file a color drawing with a statement that "no claim is made to color" or "color is not a feature of the mark." If this occurs, the examining attorney must require the applicant to claim color as a feature of the mark. The applicant may not substitute a black-and-white drawing, unless the examining attorney determines that color is non-material.

AUTHOR'S COMMENTS
About: "The USPTO does not endorse or recommend any one commercial color identification system."

Most graphic designers use the Pantone Matching System (PMS) in selecting colors and the USPTO, when soliciting a bid on outside contracting for color prints, require the contractors use of PMS matching.

807.07(D)   COLOR DRAWINGS THAT CONTAIN BLACK, WHITE, OR GRAY

When color is claimed as a feature of the mark, the applicant must submit a color claim that identifies each color and a separate color location statement describing where each color appears in the mark. 37 C.F.R §2.52(b)(1); TMEP §§807.07(a)–807.07(a)(ii). The applicant must claim all colors shown in the mark; the applicant cannot claim color for some elements of the mark and not others. See id. For example, when the drawing includes solid black lettering as well as elements in other colors, the applicant must claim the color black as a feature of the mark and include reference to the black lettering in the color location statement. The applicant may not state that solid black lettering represents all colors, or that it represents the particular color of the label, product, packaging, advertisement, website, or other specimen on which the mark appears at any given time.

If color is claimed as a feature of the mark, the drawing may include black, white, and/or gray used in two ways: (1) as claimed features of the mark; and/or (2) as a means to depict a certain aspect of the mark that is not a feature of the mark, such as broken- or dotted-line outlining to show placement of the mark on a product or package; to represent shading or stippling; to depict depth or three-dimensional shape; or to indicate areas that are not part of the mark, such as background or transparent areas. SeeTMEP §§807.08, 808.01(b).

The terms "background" and "transparent areas" refer to the white or black portions of the drawing which are not part of the mark, but appear or will appear in the particular color of the label, product, packaging, advertisement, website, or other acceptable specimen on which the mark is or will be displayed. The applicant may not claim that the background or transparent areas represent all colors or that they represent the particular color of the label, product, packaging, advertisement, website, or other specimen on which the mark appears at any given time.

If the applicant claims color as a feature of the mark, the examining attorney must require the applicant to:

• state that the color(s) black, white, and/or gray (and all other colors in the drawing) are claimed as a feature of the mark, and describe where the color(s) appear(s) on the mark; or

• if appropriate, state that the black, white, and/or gray in the drawing represents background, outlining, shading, and/or transparent areas and is not part of the mark

These statement(s) may be submitted in either a written amendment to the application or by an examiner's amendment. The examining attorney must ensure that the statement(s) is entered into the Trademark database. The statement(s) will be printed on the registration certificate.

The only exception to the requirement to claim or explain any black, white, and/or gray shown on the drawing is that, if the background of the drawing is white and it is clear that the white background is not part of the mark, no explanation of the white background is required. For example, if the drawing depicts the letters "ABC" in solid blue on a white background, or depicts a solid purple and green flower on a white background, no statement about the white background is required. On the other hand, if the shape of each of the letters "ABC" is outlined in blue with an enclosed white interior, or if the purple and green flower is enclosed in a green or black rectangle, square, or circle with a white interior, the applicant must explain the purpose of the interior white areas on the drawing.

807.07(d)(i)   Applications Under §1

If the drawing includes black, white, gray tones, gray shading, and/or gray stippling, and also includes other colors (e.g., red, turquoise, and beige), and the color claim does not include the black/white/gray, the examining attorney must require the applicant to either: (1) add the black/white/gray to the color claim and to the color location statement; or (2) if appropriate, add a statement that "The <black/white/gray> in the drawing represents background, outlining, shading, and/or transparent areas and is not part of the mark."

Drawing must match the specimen of use. The drawing of the mark must be a substantially exact representation of the mark as used on or in connection with the goods/services, as shown by the specimen. 37 C.F.R. §2.51(a)–(b); see 37 C.F.R. §2.72(a)(1), (b)(1); TMEP §§807.12(a)–807.12(a)(iii).

For example, if the drawing shows a red flower and the letters XYZ in the color black, the specimen must show the mark in the same colors. If the specimen depicts the lettering in a color other than solid black (e.g., green), the applicant must: (1) submit an amended drawing that depicts the lettering in the color shown on the specimen, if the amendment would not materially alter the mark; and (2) amend the color claim and the color location statement to match the new drawing, e.g., replace the word "black" with the word "green." Alternatively, the applicant may submit a substitute specimen showing use of the mark In the colors depicted on the drawing, or, if deleting the colors from the drawing would not materially alter the mark, the applicant may delete the color claim and substitute a black-and-white drawing for the color drawing. 37 C.F.R. §2.72.

807.07(e)   Black-and-White Drawings and Color Claims

If an applicant submits a black-and-white drawing that is lined for color (see TMEP §808.01(b)), or if the applicant submits a black-and-white drawing with an application that includes a color claim, the examining attorney must require the applicant to submit a color drawing, a claim that color(s) is a feature of the mark, and a separate statement naming the color(s) and describing where the color(s) appears on the mark.   See TMEP §§807.07(a)–807.07(a)(ii). If, however, the examining attorney determines that the color is a non-material element of the drawing, the applicant may instead be given the option of submitting a black-and-white drawing that is not lined for color, or deleting the color claim in the written application, whichever is applicable.

If an applicant submits a black-and-white drawing that is not lined for color, and there is no color claim in the written application, generally the applicant cannot substitute a color drawing and claim color, unless the examining attorney determines that the color is a non-material element of the drawing.

807.07(F)   BLACK-AND-WHITE DRAWINGS THAT CONTAIN GRAY OR BLACK-AND-WHITE DRAWINGS WITH A MARK DESCRIPTION THAT REFERS TO BLACK, WHITE, OR GRAY

807.07(F)(I)   TEAS, TEAS RF, TEAS PLUS, AND §66(A) APPLICATIONS

If the applicant submits a black-and-white drawing that contains gray or stippling that produces gray tones, and the application states that color is not claimed as a feature of the mark, no further inquiry is required. Similarly, if an applicant submits a black-and-white drawing and a description of the mark that references black, white, and/or gray, and the applicant states that color is not claimed as a feature of the mark, no further inquiry is required and no change to the description of the mark is required.

The word "No" in the "Color Mark" field on a TEAS, TEAS RF, or TEAS Plus application, or in the "Mark in Color" field on a §66(a) application, is sufficient to indicate that color is not claimed as a feature of the mark, even if the application contains the notation "grayscale" in reference to the drawing.

> When a mark contains stippling, it is generally not necessary to require a statement that the stippling represents shading or is a feature of the mark, unless the examining attorney believes such a statement is necessary to accurately describe the mark. See TMEP §808.01(b) regarding stippling statements.

> **AUTHOR'S COMMENTS**
> Yes, black and white are colors!
> Many IP Attorneys ask this question.

807.08 Broken Lines to Show Placement

37 C.F.R. §2.52(b)(4) Broken lines to show placement.

If necessary to adequately depict the commercial impression of the mark, the applicant may be required to submit a drawing that shows the placement of the mark by surrounding the mark with a proportionately accurate broken-line representation of the particular goods, packaging, or advertising on which the mark appears. The applicant must also use broken lines to show any other matter not claimed as part of the mark. For any drawing using broken lines to indicate placement of the mark, or matter not claimed as part of the mark, the applicant must describe the mark and explain the purpose of the broken lines.

Occasionally, the position of the mark on the goods, packaging, or a label may be a feature of the mark. If necessary to adequately depict the commercial impression of the mark, the examining attorney may require the applicant to submit a drawing that shows the placement of the mark by surrounding the mark with a proportionately accurate broken- or dotted-line representation of the particular goods, packaging, or advertising on which the mark appears. The applicant must also use broken or dotted lines to show any other matter not claimed as part of the mark. For any drawing using broken or dotted lines to indicate placement of the mark, or matter not claimed as part of the mark, the applicant must include a written description of the mark and explain the purpose of the broken or dotted lines, for example, by indicating that the matter shown by the broken or dotted lines is not a part of the mark and that it serves only to show the position of the mark. 37 C.F.R. §2.52(b)(4).

The drawing should clearly define the matter the applicant claims as its mark. See In re Water Gremlin Co., 635 F.2d 841, 208 USPQ 89 (C.C.P.A. 1980) ; In re Famous Foods, Inc., 217 USPQ 177 (TTAB 1983).

See TMEP §1202.02(c)(i) regarding drawings of three-dimensional trade dress marks.

Because the matter depicted in broken or dotted lines is not part of the mark, it should not be considered in determining likelihood of confusion. In re Homeland Vinyl Prods, Inc., 81 USPQ2d 1378 (TTAB 2006). See TMEP §1202.02(c)(i) regarding drawings in trade dress applications.

807.10   Three-Dimensional Marks

37 C.F.R. §2.52(b)(2) Three dimensional marks.

If the mark has three-dimensional features, the drawing must depict a single rendition of the mark, and the applicant must indicate that the mark is three-dimensional.
If the mark is three-dimensional, the drawing should present a single rendition of the mark in three dimensions.   See In re Schaefer Marine, Inc., 223 USPQ 170, 171 n.1 (TTAB 1984). The applicant must include a description of the mark indicating that the mark is three-dimensional.

Under 37 C.F.R. §2.52(b)(2), the applicant is required to submit a drawing that depicts a single rendition of the mark.   See TMEP §1202.02(c)(iv). If the applicant believes that its mark cannot be adequately depicted in a single rendition, the applicant may file a petition under 37 C.F.R. §2.146 requesting that the rule be waived. See TMEP Chapter 1700 regarding petitions, and TMEP §1202.02(c)(ii) regarding information required in descriptions for trade dress marks comprising product design or product packaging, or trade dress for services.

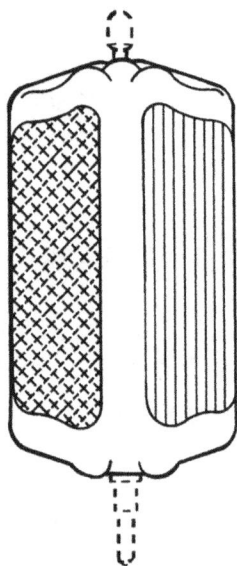

AUTHOR'S COMMENTS

Example of a 3-D Mark
I made the drawing and gave it a slight perspective to give you a feeling of three dimensions, rather than to make the drawing a flat side view.

Description of Mark: The mark consists of a configuration mark which is a three-sided reflective rotor mounted on a rotating shaft, The dotted portion of the mark and is not part of the mark. The mark is lined for the colors red and orange with the framing in white.
Note: Lining for colors is no longer used.

807.11   MARKS WITH MOTION

37 C.F.R. §2.52(b)(3)   Motion marks.

If the mark has motion, the drawing may depict a single point in the movement, or the drawing may depict up to five freeze frames showing various points in the movement, whichever best depicts the commercial impression of the mark. The applicant must also describe the mark.

If the mark includes motion (i.e., a repetitive motion of short duration) as a feature, the applicant may submit a drawing that depicts a single point in the movement, or the applicant may submit a square drawing that contains up to five freeze frames showing various points in the movement, whichever best depicts the commercial impression of the mark. The applicant must also submit a detailed written description of the mark. 37 C.F.R. §2.52(b)(3).

See TMEP §904.03(l) regarding specimens for motion marks.

AUTHOR'S COMMENTS

It is very hard to illustrate "five freeze frames" in the allowable space of a 3-inch square. Most marks with motion applications choose "a single point." In specimens 904.03(l) "an acceptable specimen should show the whole repetitive motion." (e.g., a video clip, a series of still photos, or a series of screen shots).

One of the oldest and best known *marks with motion* is the MGM roaring lion that has a long history, created in 1916 with first use in 1917 in black and white films. The MGM Roaring Lion has had many changes through its 104 years but the roaring lion is still there.

Word Mark: MGM Television, Metro Goldwyn Mayer ARS GRATIA ARTIS Trademark.
Translation: The English translation of "ARS GRATIA ARTIS" in the mark is "ART FOR THE SAKE OF ART."
Mark Drawing Code: (3) Design plus Words, Letters and/or Numbers.
Serial Number: 5880553 **Registration Number:** 4744119
Owner: (Registrant) Metro-Goldwyn-Mayer Lion Corp.
Attorney of Record: Michael B. Moore
Type of Mark: Service Mark
Live/Dead Indicator: Live
> *Author's Note: The original reproduction of this mark is in color.*

807.18 Mark Drawing Code

Standard Character Drawings. Standard character drawings are coded in the USPTO's automated system as mark drawing code 4. Prior to November 2, 2003, typed drawings (see TMEP §807.03(i)) were coded as mark drawing code 1. Mark drawing code 1 is not available for applications filed on or after November 2, 2003. Applications that were filed before November 2, 2003, may be amended to mark drawing code 1, if appropriate for that drawing. Only mark drawing code 4 should be used for standard character drawings.

Special Form Drawings. Marks comprising only a design are coded as mark drawing code 2; marks comprising words plus a design are coded as mark drawing code 3; and marks comprising stylized letters and/or numerals with no design feature are coded as mark drawing code 5. All marks consisting of words, numerals, and/or diacritical symbols for which no standard character claim (see TMEP §807.03(a)) has been submitted are coded as mark drawing code 5.

Non-Visual Marks. "Drawings" of non-visual marks (see TMEP §807.09) are coded as mark drawing code 6.

CODE:	DESCRIPTION:
1	Typed drawings prior to November 2, 2003
2	Special Form Drawing: Design Only
3	Special Form Drawing: Design plus Words/Numbers
4	Standard Character Drawings
5	Special Form Drawing: Stylized Letters and Numerals
6	Non-Visual Marks

808.01(b) Lining and Stippling Statements for Drawings

Current Practice. For applications filed on or after November 2, 2003, the USPTO does not accept black-and-white drawings lined for color. 37 C.F.R. §2.52(b)(1); TMEP §807.07(a). Thus, the examining attorney should not require the applicant to enter a statement that the lining or stippling represents shading or is a feature of the mark, unless the examining attorney believes such a statement is necessary to accurately describe the mark.

See TMEP §§808.03 et seq. and 817 regarding printing of lining and stippling statements and other descriptions of the mark.

Previous Practice. Prior to October 30, 1999, an applicant who wanted to show color in a mark was required to use the USPTO's color lining system. The color lining system required applicants to line their drawings using certain patterns designated for certain colors, and to provide a color lining statement describing where the colors appeared.

The color lining system was deleted from the rule effective October 30, 1999; however, during a transitional period between October 30, 1999 and November 2, 2003, the USPTO continued to accept drawings that showed color by using this lining system. See 64 Fed. Reg. 48900, 48903 (Sept. 8, 1999), 1226 TMOG 103, 106 (Sept. 28, 1999). When an applicant submitted a drawing that included lining that was a feature of the mark and was not intended to indicate color, the applicant was required to submit a statement to that effect, so the record would be clear as to what applicant was claiming as the mark. Similarly, when an applicant submitted a drawing that included stippling for shading purposes, the applicant was required to submit a statement to that effect.

819.01(i)   Drawing

The application must include a clear drawing of the mark comprising either: (1) a claim of standard characters and the mark, typed in the appropriate TEAS Plus field; or (2) a digitized image of a mark in special form. 37 C.F.R. §2.22(a)(12). TEAS Plus requires the applicant to indicate whether the mark is stylized or in standard characters, and will not accept the transmission unless the applicant selects one of these options. If the applicant claims standard characters, TEAS Plus will not accept transmission unless something has been typed in the appropriate field. The TEAS Plus system will generate a digitized image of the standard character mark and attach it to the application.

A "clear drawing of the mark" is the same standard used in 37 C.F.R. §2.21(a)(3), which sets forth the requirements for receipt of an application filing date. Thus, if the TEAS Plus application does not include a clear drawing of the mark, the application will be denied a filing date, in accordance with standard procedures for processing informal applications (see TMEP §§202–202.03 and 204–204.03). If the application meets the requirement for a clear drawing of the mark, the applicant will not lose TEAS Plus status if the examining attorney requires amendment of the drawing because it does not meet all the requirements of 37 C.F.R. §§2.51–2.53.

Marks That Include Color. If the mark includes color, the drawing must show the mark in color, or the applicant will lose TEAS Plus status. 37 C.F.R. §2.22(a)(12). The application must also include a color claim and a statement in the "Description of the Mark" field naming the color(s) and describing where they appear on the mark. 37 C.F.R. §§2.22(a)(14) and 2.52(b)(1).   See TMEP §819.01(j).

See TMEP §§807.03–807.03(i) for further information about standard character drawings, and TMEP §807.05(c) for the requirements for digitized images.

819.01(J)   COLOR CLAIM

As noted above, if the mark includes color, the drawing must show the mark in color. 37 C.F.R. §2.22(a)(12). In addition, the application must include: (1) a claim that the color(s) is a feature of the mark; and (2) a statement in the "Description of the Mark" field naming the color(s) and describing where the color(s) appear on the mark. 37 C.F.R. §§2.22(a)(14) and 2.52(b)(1). The TEAS Plus form includes a checkbox in the "Color(s) Claimed" field to indicate whether the mark is in color. When the applicant checks this box, the applicant must name the colors claimed in the text field below the checkbox in the same "Color(s) Claimed" field. The applicant must then enter the color location statement in a separate "Description of the Mark" field.

As long as the initial application has a color drawing and applicant makes a reasonable attempt to identify the colors claimed in either the "Color(s) Claimed" field or the "Description of the Mark" field, no additional fee is required if the application is amended to clarify the information or to correct an inadvertent error, as long as the amendment is filed through TEAS or entered by examiner's amendment. For example, applicant will not lose TEAS Plus status if the list of colors claimed is incomplete, or if the mark description does not identify the location of the colors claimed. However, the additional fee is required if the applicant fails to identify any colors.

See TMEP §§807.07(a)–807.07(a)(ii) for further information about color claims.

819.01(K)   DESCRIPTION OF THE MARK

If the mark is not in standard characters, the application must include a description of the mark. 37 C.F.R. §§2.22(a)(15) and 2.37. The applicant must enter the description in the "Description of the Mark" field of the TEAS Plus application.

TEAS Plus will not accept transmission of an application that does not include either: (1) a standard character claim; or (2) a description of the mark. If the applicant makes a good faith effort to describe the mark, no additional fee is required if the description is later amended, either in response to an examining attorney's requirement or on applicant's initiative, as long as the amendment is filed through TEAS or entered by examiner's amendment. However, the additional fee is required if the applicant enters completely inappropriate information in the "Description of the Mark" field.

If the mark includes color, the "Description of the Mark" field must include a statement naming the color(s) and describing where the color(s) appear on the mark. See TMEP §819.01(j) regarding color claims.

See TMEP §§808–808.03(g) for further information about descriptions of the mark.

TMEP Chapter 0900

Use in Commerce
(Specimens)

Remember, though, that the specimens for goods and the specimens for services are not the same. Goods specimens show the mark on the goods, the labeling, or the packaging; services specimens show the mark in the advertising or providing of the services.

Also remember, it is not enough to show how you might use a specimen in the marketplace. You must submit a photograph, screenshot, or similar representation of the actual thing.
Mock-ups and digitally altered specimens are not acceptable.

And, as before, remember that a specimen is not the same thing as a drawing. A drawing shows what the mark is; a specimen shows how the mark is used.
Source: USPTO Video

Specimens, use in commerce

The two most common filing bases are Section 1(a) Use-in-Commerce and Section 1(b) Intent-to-Use. Section 1(a) is for when you are already using your mark in interstate commerce. Section 1(b) is for when you are not yet using the mark in interstate commerce, but you have a bona fide intent to do so within the next 3-4 years.

The easiest way to think about it is this: a specimen shows how you actually use the mark in commerce in connection with your goods and services. It's real-life evidence of how the public encounters your mark in the marketplace. And the specimen you submit must be acceptable to the USPTO. *Source: USPTO*

Specimens submitted along with the trademark application's graphic image have changed recently do to the tech industry. Where a "special form trademark" is generally created by a graphic designer by using hand tools then scanned or it is created by a computer drawing or graphics software, as long as it can be "saved as" a JPG image and the size requirements to satisfy the USPTO and/or WIPO's Madrid rules.
Simply put, they do not care how the special form trademark is created.

Now comes the problem of trademark examiner rejections [of specimen's use in commerce images] that may appear like they have been "Photo Shopped" created instead of the "real thing," this why I have included Example 1 through 11 on pages 71 through 86. Although these examples are mostly for Web-pages they still give the applicant a general idea of what the examiner requires.

Ways an applicant can submit photographs of your specimen:
• Photograph your specimen sitting on a purchase order or other relevant document.
• Photograph two of your specimens, one face forward and the other back of the specimen, especially if the back has data such as bar code, price tag, etc. Set up the photo-shoot with two of the same specimens close together.
• Photograph the specimen in its place of sales environment.

Save digital photo in "raw" or TIFF if possible and submit final as a .pdf or .jpg
Whereas a trademark image can be no larger than 3 x 3 inches a specimen can be a maximum of 14 x 14 inches or smaller, 300 dpi no larger 30MB per file. (See page 30).

To complete a Section 1(a) basis, upload a JPG or PDF image of a specimen of use that shows how you are using the mark in commerce, provide a brief description of the specimen, and provide both the date of first use of the mark anywhere and the date of first use of the mark in commerce. The dates are often the same. *Source: USPTO*

Chapter 900 - Use in Commerce

904   Specimens

Specimens are required because they show the manner in which the mark is seen by the public. Specimens also provide supporting evidence of facts recited in the application.

A trademark or service mark application for registration under §1(a) of the Trademark Act must include one specimen for each class, showing use of the mark in commerce on or in connection with the goods, or in the sale or advertising of the services. 15 U.S.C. §1051(a)(1); 37 C.F.R. §§2.34(a)(1)(iv), 2.56(a). If an application under §1(a) is filed without a specimen, the examining attorney must issue an Office action requiring the applicant to submit one specimen for each class, with an affidavit or declaration under 37 C.F.R. §2.20 stating that the specimen was in use in commerce at least as early as the filing date of the application.   See 37 C.F.R. §2.59(a). The Office action must also indicate registration is refused under §§1 and 45 of the Trademark Act because the applicant has not provided evidence of use of the mark in commerce.
    See 15 U.S.C. §§1051(a)(1), 1127; 37 C.F.R. §§2.34(a)(1)(iv), 2.56(a).

In examining a specimen filed with an application under 15 U.S.C. §1051(a), an amendment to allege use under 15 U.S.C. §1051(c), or a statement of use under 15 U.S.C. §1051(d), the examining attorney must refuse registration if the specimen indicates that the goods have not been "sold or transported in commerce." 15 U.S.C. §1127. For example, a webpage for placing pre-sale orders for goods that are not yet available does not show use of the mark in commerce in connection with the goods, even if it otherwise meets the requirements for an acceptable display associated with the goods. *See Richardson-Vicks, Inc. v. Franklin Mint Corp., 216 USPQ 989, 991-92 (TTAB 1982) (finding that the goods to be identified by the mark must be in existence at the time of a sale); cf. Aycock Eng'g, Inc. v. Airflite, Inc., 560 F.3d 1350, 1360, 90 USPQ2d 1301, 1308 (Fed. Cir. 2009) (holding that actual use of the mark in commerce in connection with an existing service is required and that mere preparations to use a mark sometime in the future does not constitute use in commerce); In re Port Auth. of N.Y., 3 USPQ2d 1453, 1455 (TTAB 1987) (finding advertising and promoting telecommunications services before the services were available insufficient to support registration); In re Cedar Point, Inc., 220 USPQ 533, 535-37 (TTAB 1983) (holding that advertising of a marine entertainment park, which was not yet open, was not a valid basis for registration); In re Nationwide Mut. Ins. Co., 124 USPQ 465 (TTAB 1960) (holding that stickers placed on policies, bills, and letters announcing prospective name change is mere adoption, not* service mark use). See TMEP §1301.03 regarding use of a service mark in commerce. The Office action must indicate that registration is refused under §§1 and 45 of the Trademark Act because the applicant has not provided evidence of use of the mark in commerce for the identified goods. See 15 U.S.C. §§1051(a)(1), 1127; 37 C.F.R. §§2.34(a)(1)(iv), 2.56(a).

In an application for registration under §1(b) of the Trademark Act, no specimen is required at the time the application is filed. However, before a registration will issue, the applicant must file an allegation of use that includes one specimen for each class, showing use of the mark in commerce on or in connection with the goods or in the sale or advertising of the services. See 37 C.F.R. §§2.56(a), 2.76(b)(2), 2.88(b)(2).

No specimen showing use of the mark in commerce is required in an application based solely on §44 or §66(a) of the Trademark Act, 15 U.S.C. §§1126(d)-(e), 1141f(a). While a §44 or §66(a) applicant must assert a bona fide intent to use the mark in commerce, the applicant is not required to assert actual use in commerce prior to registration. Crocker Nat'l Bank v. Canadian Imperial Bank of Com., 223 USPQ 909 (TTAB 1984); TMEP §§1009, 1904.01(d).

If the nature of a specimen is unclear, the applicant must explain what it is and how it is used.

A photocopy or reproduction of the drawing is not an acceptable specimen. 37 C.F.R. §2.56(c).

Specimens of value should not be filed.

Interested parties, including potential opposers, may view and print images of the specimens in an application or registration file through the Trademark Status and Document Retrieval ("TSDR") portal on the USPTO website at http://tsdr.uspto.gov/. The USPTO does not permit specimens to be removed from the record. Furthermore, once filed, specimens remain part of the record and will not be returned to the applicant. 37 C.F.R. §2.25. This ensures that there is a complete record of the submissions made by the applicant. See 64 Fed. Reg. 48900, 48901 (Sept. 8, 1999), 1226 TMOG 103 (Sept. 28, 1999); see also TMEP §404.

For information regarding specimens for collective trademarks and collective service marks, see TMEP §1303.01(a)(i)(C); for collective membership marks, see TMEP §1304.02(a)(i)(C); and for certification marks, see TMEP §§1306.02(a)(i)(B), 1306.04(c)-(d).

904.01   NUMBER OF SPECIMENS

One specimen for each class is required in an application for registration under §1(a) of the Trademark Act, or in an allegation of use in an application under §1(b). If a single specimen supports multiple classes, the applicant should indicate which classes are supported by the specimen. The examining attorney need not require multiple copies of the specimen. The examining attorney should enter a Note to the File in the record indicating which class(es) the specimen supports.

904.02(a)   Electronically Filed Specimens

In an electronically filed application, allegation of use, affidavit of use under 15 U.S.C. §1058 or §1141k of the Trademark Act ("§8 affidavit" or "§71 affidavit"), or response to an Office action, the specimen(s) must be in .jpg or .pdf format. 37 C.F.R. §§2.56(d)(4), 2.161(g), 7.37(g). If the nature of the specimen is unclear, the applicant should describe what it is and how it is used. See TMEP §904.03(d) regarding electronic and digital media attachments and §904.03(f) regarding specimens for sound marks.

Sometimes, although the application indicates that a specimen is included, the specimen is not visible in the record due to a technical problem that occurred during submission of the application. In this situation, the examining attorney should first send an e-mail to the TEAS mailbox to ask whether the problem can be fixed by uploading the file again. If it cannot, the examining attorney must request that the applicant submit: (1) the same specimen (or a true copy) that was attached to the original TEAS submission; and (2) a statement by the person who transmitted the original TEAS submission that the specimen being submitted is a true copy of the specimen originally filed through TEAS. This statement does not have to be verified. Alternatively, the applicant may submit a different specimen from that initially filed, together with an affidavit or declaration of use of the substitute specimen. See TMEP §904.05 regarding the requirements for an affidavit or declaration supporting use of substitute specimens.

The USPTO prefers that the specimen, whether a true copy of the original or a substitute, be submitted electronically via the Trademark Electronic Application System ("TEAS"). In TEAS, the Response to Office Action form can be accessed by clicking on the link entitled "Response Forms" at http://www.uspto.gov.

904.02(c)(ii)   Specimens for Marks Comprising Color

If color is a feature of the mark, or if the mark consists solely of color, the specimen must show use of the color. 37 C.F.R. §2.51; TMEP §807.12. Note: In an application filed on or after November 2, 2003, if an applicant submits a color drawing, or a description of the mark that indicates the use of color on the mark, the applicant must claim color as a feature of the mark. 37 C.F.R. §2.52(b)(1); TMEP §807.07(a)(i).

If the applicant submits a specimen that is not in color or not in the appropriate color, the examining attorney will require the applicant to file a substitute specimen that shows use of the appropriate color(s). See TMEP §904.05 regarding substitute specimens.

See also TMEP §1202.05(f) regarding specimens showing use of marks that consist solely of color.

904.02(c)(iii)   SPECIMENS FOR MARKS USED ON PUBLICATIONS

An application for registration of a mark for publications is treated the same as any other application with respect to specimen requirements. The USPTO does not require a complete copy of the publication or a title page in every case. However, the examining attorney may require a copy of the publication under 37 C.F.R. §2.61(b) if he or she believes it is necessary for proper examination. For example, a copy of the publication might be necessary to determine whether a mark is merely descriptive of the goods.

904.03   MATERIAL APPROPRIATE AS SPECIMENS FOR TRADEMARKS

For a trademark application under §1(a), allegation of use in an application under §1(b), or affidavit of use under §8 or §71 of the Trademark Act, the specimen must show the mark as used on or in connection with the goods in commerce. A trademark specimen should be a label, tag, or container for the goods, or a display associated with the goods. 37 C.F.R. §2.56(b)(1). A photocopy or other reproduction of a specimen of the mark as used on or in connection with the goods is acceptable. 37 C.F.R. §2.56(c).

See TMEP §§1301.04 et seq. regarding service mark specimens, TMEP §1304.02(a)(i)(C) regarding collective membership mark specimens, TMEP §1303.01(a)(i)(C) regarding collective trademark and collective service mark specimens, and TMEP §1306.02(a)(i)(B) regarding certification mark specimens.

904.03(a)　Labels and Tags

In most cases, if a trademark is ordinarily applied to the goods or the containers for the goods by means of labels, a label is an acceptable specimen. However, if a mark is merely informational or incapable of functioning as a mark for some other reason, it would not be seen as an indicator of source, and registration must be refused even if the specimen of record shows what would otherwise be acceptable trademark use, including use on tags or labels. SeeTMEP §1202.04.

Shipping or mailing labels may be accepted if they are affixed to the goods or to the containers for the goods and if proper trademark usage is shown.　In re A.S. Beck Shoe Corp., 161 USPQ 168 (TTAB 1969); Elec. Commc'ns, Inc. v. Elec. Components for Indus. Co., 443 F.2d 487, 170 USPQ 118 (8th Cir. 1971).　They are not acceptable if the mark as shown is merely used as a trade name and not as a trademark. An example of this is the use of the term solely as a return address.　In re Supply Guys, Inc., 86 USPQ2d 1488 (TTAB 2008); Bookbinder's Sea Food House, Inc. v. Book-binder's Rest., Inc., 118 USPQ 318 (Comm'r Pats. 1958); I. & B. Cohen Bomzon & Co. v. Biltmore Indus., Inc., 22 USPQ 257 (Comm'r Pats. 1934).　See TMEP §1202.01 regarding trade name refusals.

For labels or tags whose appearance suggests that they are not in actual use in commerce, the examining attorney may, under 37 C.F.R. §2.61(b), inquire as to how the specimen is used in order to properly examine the application.　For example, an inquiry may be appropriate when the specimen consists of a photograph of the mark reproduced on a plain white label adhered to the goods or printed packaging or a piece of paper bearing the mark placed on top of the goods or packaging. If, based on the available evidence, the examining attorney determines that the specimen is not in actual use in commerce, registration may be refused on that basis instead of issuing an inquiry. See TMEP §904.07(a).　However, nothing prohibits the registration of a mark in an application that contains only "temporary" specimens, provided that the specimens were actually used in commerce.　See In re Chica, 84 USPQ2d 1845,1847-48 (TTAB 2007) (finding applicant's specimen unacceptable not because it was temporary but because it comprised a mere drawing of the goods with an illustration of how the mark may be displayed and not an actual specimen that applicant used in commerce).

See TMEP §904.04(a) regarding digitally created or altered specimens and §904.07(a) regarding "use-in-commerce" issues that may be raised on initial review of specimens.

904.03(c)   Commercial Packaging

The terminology "applied to the containers for the goods" means applied to any type of commercial packaging that is normal for the particular goods as they move in trade. Thus, a showing of the trademark on the normal commercial package for the particular goods is an acceptable specimen.   *In re Brown Jordan Co.*, 219 USPQ 375 (TTAB 1983) (holding that stamping the mark after purchase of the goods, on a tag attached to the goods that are later transported in commerce, is sufficient use). For example, gasoline pumps are normal containers or "packaging" for gasoline.

A specimen showing use of the trademark on a vehicle in which the goods are marketed to the relevant purchasers may constitute use of the mark on a container for the goods, if this is the normal mode of use of a mark for the particular goods. *In re E.A. Miller & Sons Packing Co.*, 225 USPQ 592 (TTAB 1985). *But see In re Lyndale Farm,* 186 F.2d 723, 88 USPQ 377 (C.C.P.A. 1951).

904.03(d)   ELECTRONIC AND DIGITAL MEDIA ATTACHMENTS TO PAPER FILINGS

In the absence of alternative specimens, the USPTO will accept specimens consisting of compact discs ("CDs"), digital video discs ("DVDs"), videotapes, and audiotapes. See 37 C.F.R. §2.56(d)(3). Equipment for viewing or listening to these materials is available at the USPTO.

Compact discs, DVDs, audiotapes, and videotapes may contain files in .jpg, .pdf, .wav, .wmv, .wma, .mp3, .mpg, or .avi format. The USPTO is unable to review files in any other format. The USPTO prefers that the applicant submit small files of less than two minutes in duration. Only one specimen should be included on each tape or disc; however, in a multiple-class application, the applicant may include more than one specimen on the same disc or tape. If the nature of the specimen is unclear, the applicant should explain what it is and how it is used.

See TMEP §904.02(a) regarding electronically filed specimens, TMEP §904.03(f) regarding specimens for sound marks, and TMEP §904.03(l) regarding specimens for motion marks. See also 37 C.F.R. §§2.56(d)(1) and (d)(2) and TMEP §904.02(b) regarding the size requirements for specimens attached to paper filings, and the procedures for handling specimens that exceed these requirements.

904.03(i) Electronic Displays

A web page that displays a product can constitute a "display associated with the goods" if it:

- • (1) contains a picture or textual description of the identified goods;
- • (2) shows the mark in association with the goods; and
- • (3) provides a means for ordering the identified goods.

See In re Sones, 590 F.3d 1282, 1288, 93 USPQ2d 1118, 1123 (Fed Cir. 2009); In re Azteca Sys., Inc., 102 USPQ2d 1955, 1957-58 (TTAB 2012) ; In re Dell Inc., 71 US-PQ2d 1725, 1727 (TTAB 2004) ; *Lands' End v. Manbeck,* 797 F. Supp. 511, 514, 24 USPQ2d 1314, 1316 (E.D. Va. 1992).

The mark must also be displayed on the web page in a manner in which customers will recognize it as a mark. *See In re Morganroth,* 208 USPQ 284, 287-88 (TTAB 1980) ; *see also In re Osterberg,* 83 USPQ2d 1220, 1223 (TTAB 2007) (finding that CONDOM-TOY CONDOM was not displayed so prominently on web page specimen that consumers would recognize it as a trademark for condoms). See TMEP §1202.04 regarding matter that is merely informational in nature.

Generally, a web page will display the trademark in association with a picture of the goods. However, in *Sones,* the Federal Circuit held that although a visual depiction of the goods "is an important consideration in determining whether a submitted specimen sufficiently associates a mark with the source of the goods," a picture of the goods on the web page is not mandatory. *In re Sones* at 1288, 93 USPQ2d at 1123. A textual description may suffice where "the actual features or inherent characteristics of the goods are recognizable from the textual description, given that the more standard the product is, the less comprehensive the textual description need be." *Id.* at 1289, 93 USPQ2d at 1124

An applicant need not describe a web-page specimen as a "display" for it to qualify as an acceptable display specimen, nor must the web page come from an applicant's own website. A web page from a third-party website may be acceptable as a display if the mark is sufficiently associated with the applicant's goods. *See In re Osterberg,* 83 USPQ2d at1221, 1223-24 (finding the specimen unacceptable not because it was a web page from a third-party website, but because it neither showed the mark in association with the goods nor provided a means for ordering the goods). For instance, a manufacturer of bed linens may rely on a third-party retail vendor's web page when the web page shows a picture of the bed linens in association with the mark and provides a means for ordering them, as shown in Example 1 on the following page.

Example 1: Mark is associated with the goods, goods are pictured and described, and ordering information is provided.

Mark: LACOSTE

Goods: Coverlets, duvet covers, duvets, bed blankets, bed linen, bed sheets, pillow cases, bath linen, washing mitts.

• The mark is placed below the website navigation tabs and is prominently displayed.

• The mark is physically close to the goods and is repeated in the links located under each product, indicating a direct association with the goods.

• No other marks appear to be used in connection with the goods apart from the alligator design and the product style names, all of which are associated with the goods.

• Product information is provided in the form of pictures and descriptions of the goods along with prices.

• There is a "shopping bag" at the top of the web page to enable direct ordering.

• Even if the web page did not include the larger LACOSTE mark, the LACOSTE marks depicted under the photographs of the goods (e.g., Lacoste "Brighton" Comforter Set or Lacoste "Confetti" Comforter Set) would be acceptable to show trademark use for the goods.

• If the proposed mark were "Macy's" (as it appears in the upper-left corner), the web page would not be acceptable for goods because of the closer proximity and association of the other marks with the goods (i.e., the LACOSTE and alligator).

Similarly, a web page from a third–party, social-media website may also be accepted provided the web page satisfies the elements of a display specimen.

+--+
| AUTHOR'S COMMENTS |
| Examples 1 through 11 have a graphic that goes with them |
| in the TMEP but I am only using the descriptions on these |
| 11 examples to give you a picture of what the USPTO |
| trademark examiners are looking for when you use a |
| capture of a web-page for your specimens. |
| This is very popular at the present time. |
+--+

However, while a web page display associated with the goods is an acceptable specimen for goods, mere advertising material is not. *In re Anpath Grp.*, 95 USPQ2d 1377, 1380 (TTAB 2010) ; *In re Quantum Foods, Inc.*, 94 USPQ2d 1375, 1379 (TTAB 2010); *In re Osterberg,* 83 USPQ2d at 1224; *In re Dell Inc.*, 71 USPQ2d at 1727; *In re MediaShare Corp.,* 43 USPQ2d 1304, 1307 (TTAB 1997) . Acceptable web-page displays are not merely advertising, but instead serve as point-of-sale displays, because the website on which the web page appears is, in effect, an electronic retail store, and the web page is a shelf-talker or banner which encourages the consumer to buy the product and provides the information necessary to do so. A consumer using the link on the web page to purchase the goods is the equivalent of a consumer seeing a shelf-talker and taking the item to the cashier in a store to purchase it. *See In re Dell Inc.*, 71 USPQ2d at 1727. The web page is, thus, a point-of-sale display by which an actual sale is made.

A point-of-sale display is "'calculated to consummate a sale'"; that is, it includes the information necessary for the consumer to decide to purchase the goods, and it appears in a setting that allows the consumer to immediately buy the goods. *In re Quantum Foods, Inc.*, 94 USPQ2d at 1379 (quoting *In re Bright of Am., Inc.*, 205 USPQ 63, 71 (TTAB 1979)); *In re Anpath Grp.*, 95 USPQ2d at 1382; *In re MediaShare Corp.*, 43 USPQ2d at 1305; *Lands' End Inc.*, 797 F. Supp. at 514, 24 USPQ2d at 1316. An advertisement, however, merely describes or touts the benefits of the goods, influences people to buy them, or informs the public about the goods and the company that provides them. *In re Anpath Grp.*, 95 USPQ2d at 1381-82; *In re Quantum Foods, Inc.*, 94 USPQ2d at 1379. It does not offer a way to directly purchase the goods, because it either does not contain an offer to accept orders for the goods or does not provide special instructions for placing orders for the goods. *In re Quantum Foods, Inc.*, 94 USPQ2d at 1380; *In re Osterberg,* 83 USPQ2d at 1224.

Therefore, a web page that merely provides information about the goods, but does not provide a means of ordering them, is viewed as promotional material, which is not acceptable to show trademark use on goods. *See In re Genitope Corp.*, 78 USPQ2d 1819, 1822 (TTAB 2006) ("[T]he company name, address and phone number that appears at the end of the web page indicates only location information about applicant; it does not constitute a means to order goods through the mail or by telephone, in the way that a catalog sales form provides a means for one to fill out a sales form or call in a purchase by phone."). Merely providing a link to the websites of online distributors is not sufficient. There must be a means of ordering the goods directly from the applicant's web page, such as a telephone number for placing orders or an online ordering process. *In re Quantum Foods, Inc.*, 94 USPQ2d at 1380; *In re Osterberg,* 83 USPQ2d at 1224.

When a web-page specimen appears to be merely advertising, statements by the applicant that the specimen is used in connection with the sale of the goods, without evidence or a detailed explanation of the manner of use, will not suffice to establish that the specimen is a display associated with the goods. *In re Osterberg,* 83 USPQ2d at 1224 (finding that applicant's mere statement in a signed declaration that copies of the web page were distributed at sales presentation lacked sufficient detail to transform the web page from an advertisement into a display associated with the goods).

Whether a web-page display qualifies as an acceptable specimen is a question of fact, based on the evidence of record. *In re Azteca Sys.,* Inc., 102 USPQ2d at 1957 (citing *Lands' End,* 797 F. Supp. at 514, 24 USPQ2d at 1316); *In re Hydron Techs. Inc.,* 51 USPQ2d 1531, 1533 (TTAB 1999). The presentation on the web page of the picture or description of the goods, the manner of the mark's use in association with those goods, and the nature of the ordering information affect the specimen's acceptability. Thus, a specimen that describes or displays a picture of the goods, shows the mark, and provides ordering information may nonetheless be unacceptable because it fails to demonstrate an association between the mark and the goods. Sometimes, a single fact or piece of evidence may be dispositive. Often, however, a combination of facts and evidence of record may be required to establish the acceptability of the specimen. If ordering information is not readily discernible from the submitted web page, the applicant may provide multiple, sequential web pages as part of the specimen to clarify the ordering process on the website.

See TMEP §904.03(i)(A)–(i)(C)(3) for further discussion of the various factors for assessing whether a web-page display is an acceptable specimen.

904.03(I)(A)   PICTURE OR DESCRIPTION OF THE GOODS

In order for a display to be associated with the goods, something on the web page must show or describe the goods for the consumer, that is, a picture or description of the goods. *See In re Sones,* 590 F.3d 1282, 1288-89, 93 USPQ2d 1118, 1123-24 (Fed. Cir. 2009). A description will suffice if "the actual features or inherent characteristics of the goods are recognizable from the textual description." *Id. at* 1289, 93 USPQ2d at 1124. The level of detail required depends on the type of goods at issue. *Id.* Standard products (e.g., television sets, baseball gloves, or pet food) typically will not require a comprehensive description for the consumer to know what the goods are. Complicated or sophisticated products (e.g., computer products, medical devices, or industrial machinery) may require a more detailed description, in the absence of a picture of the goods.

904.03(I)(B)   SHOW THE MARK IN ASSOCIATION WITH THE GOODS

A web-page display specimen "must in some way evince that the mark is 'associated' with the goods and serves as an indicator of source." *In re Sones,* 590 F.3d 1282, 1288, 93 USPQ2d 1118, 1123 (Fed. Cir. 2009). Assessing the "mark-goods" association on a web page involves many variables, including the prominence and placement of the mark, the content and layout of the web page, and the overall impression the web page creates. Web-page content and layout may sometimes distract consumers and prevent them from making the necessary connection between the mark and the identified goods. *In re Azteca Sys., Inc.,* 102 USPQ2d 1955, 1958 (TTAB 2012) . Factors such as the proximity of the mark to the goods, the presence of other marks, intervening text between the mark and the goods, and the inclusion of other material that is unrelated or marginally related to the identified goods, tend to disrupt purchasers from making the mark-goods association, as shown in Example 2. *Id.*

Example 2: Applied-for mark is not associated with the goods.

Mark: GIS EMPOWERED BY CITYWORKS

Goods: Computer software for management of public works and utilities assets

• THE APPLIED-FOR MARK IS DISTANT FROM THE DESCRIPTION OF THE SOFTWARE, AND IS SEPARATED FROM THE DESCRIPTION BY MORE THAN FIFTEEN LINES OF TEXT CONCERNING MARGINALLY RELATED TOPICS;

• DUE TO THE APPEARANCE OF A NUMBER OF OTHER MARKS ON THE WEB PAGE, IT IS UNCLEAR WHETHER ANY PARTICULAR MARK IS ASSOCIATED AND USED IN CONNECTION WITH THE IDENTIFIED GOODS;

• THE LEFT SIDEBAR INCLUDES LINKS TO ARTICLES AND NEWS ABOUT APPLICANT'S BUSINESS AND IS NOT LIMITED TO THE SOFTWARE GOODS.

The following features of a specimen particularly influence the mark-goods association analysis.

904.03(i)(B)(1) Prominence of Mark

When determining whether a web-page display specimen shows the mark in association with the identified goods, the examining attorney may consider the prominence of the mark. *See In re Osterberg,* 83 USPQ2d 1220, 1223 (TTAB 2007) ("Another factor in the analysis of whether a specimen is an acceptable display used in association with the goods is whether the mark is displayed in a such a way that the customer can easily associate the mark with the goods." (citing 83 USPQ2d 1220, 1223 (TTAB 2007) ("Another factor in the analysis of whether a specimen is an acceptable display used in association with the goods is whether the mark is displayed in a such a way that the customer can easily associate the mark with the goods."
(citing *In re Dell Inc.,* 71 USPQ2d 1725, 1728 (TTAB 2004)).

The more prominently an applied-for mark appears on a web page, the more likely the mark will be perceived as a trademark. A mark may appear more prominent when the specimen:

• presents the mark in larger font size or different stylization or color than the
          surrounding text;

• places the mark at the beginning of a line or sentence;

• positions the mark next to a picture or description of the goods; or

• uses the "TM" designation with the applied-for mark (however, the designation alone does not transform a mark into a trademark if other considerations indicate it does not function as a trademark).

904.03(I)(B)(2)   PLACEMENT OF MARK AND PROXIMITY TO THE GOODS

Appearance in Website and E-mail Addresses . When a mark appears in the computer browser area as part of the URL, Internet address, or domain name of the website that houses the web page, consumers generally do not recognize this as trademark use. Instead, this use merely identifies the Internet location of the website where business is conducted and goods or services are offered. *See, e.g., In re Roberts,* 87 USPQ2d 1474, 1479-80 (TTAB 2008) (concluding that the mark IRESTMYCASE, which appeared as part of a website address, www.irestmycase.com, on applicant's specimens, merely served as a contact address to reach the applicant and failed to function as a service mark for applicant's services); In re Supply Guys, Inc., 86 USPQ2d 1488, 1493 (TTAB 2008) ("[A]pplicant's use of the term LEADING EDGE TONERS as part of the internet address, www.leadingedgetoners.com, . . . identifies the website where applicant con-ducts its retail sales services. Obviously, a website can be used for multiple purposes and the simple fact that a term is used as part of the internet address does not mean that it is a trademark for the goods sold on the website."); *In re Eilberg,* 49 USPQ2d 1955, 1956 (TTAB 1998) (finding that the mark WWW.EILBERG.COM, when displayed in relatively small and subdued typeface below other contact information on applicant's letterhead, merely indicated the Internet location of applicant's website rather than functioning as a service mark for applicant's legal services). Similarly, the use of the mark embedded in an e-mail address would be viewed as part of the website address where applicant may be contacted, rather than as a trademark.

Placement in a Location Typical for a Retail-Store Service Mark . A mark may be displayed at the top of a web page, separated from the relevant goods by the website navigation tabs, which may direct consumers to information about the goods, the applicant, and the website. Since it is customary for retailers to place their store marks in this location, such use of the applied-for mark is likely be recognized as an online retail-store service mark, as shown in Example 3.

Example 3: Mark is associated with the services, but the specimen would not be acceptable as evidence of use of the mark as a trademark for the goods shown.

Mark: MACYS.COM

Services: Electronic retail department-store services

• THE WEB PAGE IS NOT ACCEPTABLE AS EVIDENCE OF USE OF THE MARK AS A TRADEMARK FOR THE GOODS SHOWN BECAUSE THE MARK IS SERVING ONLY AS A SERVICE MARK FOR RETAIL STORE SERVICES FEATURING THE GOODS OF OTHERS (E.G., "CUISINART" OR "POLO BY RALPH LAUREN").

• THE MARK IS LOCATED IN THE UPPER-LEFT CORNER WHERE RETAIL SERVICE MARKS USUALLY APPEAR AND IS ADJACENT TO THE GREETING "WELCOME TO MACYS.COM."

• OTHER TRADEMARKS FOR VARIOUS GOODS APPEAR ON THE WEB PAGE, SUCH AS "CUISINART," "CLUB ROOM," "CHARTER CLUB," AND "POLO BY RALPH LAUREN," WHICH APPEAR TO BE MORE DIRECTLY ASSOCIATED WITH THE GOODS.

• RETAIL STORE SERVICES INDICIA APPEAR, SUCH AS "DEPARTMENTS" ON THE RIGHT AND "EXPRESSCHECKOUT SIGN-IN," "BRIDAL REGISTRY," AND "WANT A CARD? GET ONE HERE" ON THE LEFT.

The mark may also include wording (e.g., "market," "store," or "depot") that indicates use as a service mark. Nevertheless, a mark appearing in a location where service marks normally appear may qualify as a trademark if the web page demonstrates an association between the applied-for mark and the identified goods, and otherwise meets the elements of an acceptable display specimen, as shown in Example 4. *See In re Supply Guys, Inc.*, 86 USPQ2d at 1495-96 (noting that "a mark may serve both as a trademark and service mark" and that one "must look to the perception of the ordinary customer to determine whether the term functions as a trademark").

Example 4: Mark is associated with the goods, goods are pictured and described, and ordering information is provided.

Mark: HAPPY SOCKS

Goods: Clothes, namely, socks

• THE MARK IS SHOWN PROMINENTLY IN THE UPPER-LEFT CORNER OF THE WEB PAGE, IS FOLLOWED BY THE "TM" DESIGNATION, IS PLACED IN CLOSE PROXIMITY TO THE GOODS, AND APPEARS TO BE THE ONLY MARK ON THE WEB PAGE ASSOCIATED WITH THE GOODS.

• THE REFERENCE TO "OUR SOCKS" UNDER "ADD TO CART" BUTTON REINFORCES TRADEMARK USE OF THE MARK BECAUSE IT CONVEYS THAT THE SOCKS SOLD ON THE WEB PAGE ARE PRODUCED BY HAPPY SOCKS.

• THE WEB PAGE CONTAINS SUFFICIENT PRODUCT DETAILS TO MAKE THE DECISION TO PURCHASE THE GOODS, INCLUDING PICTURE AND DESCRIPTION; SIZE, COLOR, AND QUANTITY OPTIONS; PRICE; AND MATERIAL CONTENT OF THE GOODS.

• THE ORDERING INFORMATION IS IN THE FORM OF AN "ADD TO CART" BUTTON ADJACENT TO THE PICTURE AND DESCRIPTION OF GOODS.

Furthermore, if a mark appears on a web page in a location where trademarks normally are not placed, a "substantially larger and more prominent" placement of the mark thereon could result in acceptable trademark use, when the only products on the web page are the identified goods, the placement of the mark is such that the mark-goods association is evident, and the web page otherwise meets the elements of an acceptable display specimen. *See Examples 5 and 6.*

Example 5: Mark is associated with the goods, goods are pictured and described, and ordering information is provided.

Mark: COLE HAAN

Goods: Eyeglasses, sunglasses, cases for spectacles and sunglasses

• THE MARK IS LOCATED IN THE UPPER-LEFT CORNER OF THE WEB PAGE AND IS PROMINENTLY DISPLAYED.

• THE MARK IS SOMEWHAT PHYSICALLY DISTANT FROM THE GOODS, BUT IT APPEARS TO BE THE ONLY MARK ON THE WEB PAGE ASSOCIATED WITH THE GOODS, AND THE ONLY PRODUCTS SHOWN ARE THE IDENTIFIED GOODS.

• ALTHOUGH THE MENU ON THE LEFT, UNDER "COLLECTIONS," DOES INCLUDE OTHER MARKS, THESE MARKS DO NOT APPEAR TO BE USED IN CONNECTION WITH THE GOODS (I.E., THE OTHER MARKS ARE NOT PLACED DIRECTLY NEXT TO THE PICTURES AND DESCRIPTIONS OF THE GOODS) AND THE MENU SIMPLY APPEARS TO INFORM CONSUMERS THAT THEY MAY ALSO PURCHASE FROM OTHER BRAND-NAME "COLLECTIONS" ON THE WEBSITE.

• ORDERING INFORMATION IN THE FORM OF A "SHOPPING BAG" IS INCLUDED NEAR THE TOP OF THE WEB PAGE.

• THE MARK MAY ALSO FUNCTION AS A SERVICE MARK FOR RETAIL STORE SERVICES SINCE THE MENU ON THE LEFT OF THE WEB PAGE CONTAINS VARIOUS CATEGORIES OF GOODS SOLD IN THE STORE, IDENTIFIES OTHER BRAND NAMES CARRIED BY THE STORE, AND PROVIDES A "STORES" LINK ON THE BOTTOM FOR LOCATING PHYSICAL STORES.

Example 6: Mark is associated with the goods, goods are pictured and described, and ordering information is provided.

Mark: BROOKS BROTHERS

Goods: Bed sheets, dust ruffles, duvet covers, pillow cases, pillow shams, bed shams, bed spreads, towels, and wash cloths

• THE MARK IS DISPLAYED PROMINENTLY IN LARGE FONT AND PLACED ABOVE THE PICTURES OF THE GOODS.

• NO OTHER MARKS APPEAR TO BE USED IN CONNECTION WITH THE IDENTIFIED GOODS APART FROM THE SHEEP DESIGN PLACED NEAR THE GOODS, WHICH IS ALSO ASSOCIATED WITH THE GOODS.

• THE WEB PAGE CONTAINS PICTURES AND DESCRIPTIONS OF THE GOODS, SIZE AND COLOR SELECTIONS, AND PRICE INFORMATION.

• THE WEB PAGE WOULD ALSO BE AN ACCEPTABLE SPECIMEN IF THE MARK WERE FOR RETAIL STORE SERVICES BECAUSE THE MARK IS LOCATED WHERE RETAIL SERVICE MARKS ARE TYPICALLY PLACED AND THE "FIND A STORE" TAB INDICATES THE PRESENCE OF PHYSICAL STORES, THUS REINFORCING SERVICE MARK USAGE.

Displayed in or Near Corporate Contact Information . A mark that appears on a web page only in conjunction with the corporate address, telephone number, and website and e-mail addresses, and/or is placed on the web page near boilerplate and standard information about the applicant or the website (e.g., "Home" and "About Us" links, legal notices, or technical requirements of the website) is less likely to be seen as a trademark and more likely to be perceived as a trade name under which the applicant conducts business. *See In re Walker Process Equip. Inc.*, 233 F.2d 329, 331-32, 110 USPQ 41, 43 (C.C.P.A. 1956) (indicating that the placement of the applied-for mark WALKER PROCESS EQUIPMENT INC. above wording denoting applicant's location suggested that the mark was not used as a trademark, but as a trade name).

Presence of Other Marks . In some instances, the appearance of more than one mark (whether word or design marks) on the web page may distract consumers and make it less likely that they will perceive an association between the applied-for mark and the relevant goods. *See In re Azteca Sys., Inc.*, 102 USPQ2d 1955, 1958 (TTAB 2012) . The placement of each mark, particularly the applied-for mark, in relation to the identified goods may affect whether it is associated with the goods and functions as a trademark (see Example 7) or, instead, serves as a service mark or trade name.

Example 7: Mark is associated with the goods, goods are pictured and described, and ordering information is provided.

Mark: KEEPING YOU COZY.

Goods: Jackets

• THE MARK IS PLACED BELOW THE WEBSITE NAVIGATION TABS AND IS PROMINENTLY DISPLAYED IN LARGE FONT FOLLOWED BY THE "TM" DESIGNATION.

• THE MARK IS PHYSICALLY CLOSE TO THE GOODS AND WOULD BE PERCEIVED TO BE ASSOCIATED WITH THEM.

• THE WEB PAGE FEATURES PRODUCT INFORMATION IN THE FORM OF PICTURES AND DESCRIPTIONS OF THE GOODS ALONG WITH PRICES.

• THE LINKS UNDER EACH PRODUCT COMBINED WITH THE "BUY ONLINE NOW!" INSTRUCTION INDICATE THAT DIRECT ORDERING IS POSSIBLE.

• IF THE PROPOSED MARK WERE "T. MARKEY YOUR CLOTHING EMPORIUM" (AS IT APPEARS IN THE UPPER-LEFT CORNER), THE WEB PAGE WOULD NOT BE ACCEPTABLE FOR GOODS BECAUSE IT IS LOCATED WHERE SERVICE MARKS ARE COMMONLY PLACED AND SEEMS TO FUNCTION AS A RETAIL STORE SERVICE MARK, THERE IS OTHER MATTER SEPARATING THE MARK FROM THE GOODS, AND THERE ARE OTHER MARKS PLACED CLOSER TO THE GOODS AND BETTER ASSOCIATED WITH THE GOODS.

The nature of the wording and design elements of each mark on the specimen and the appearance of the same or similar elements in the various marks may also influence whether the applied-for mark would be perceived as a trademark for the relevant goods, as in Example 8.

Example 8: Mark is associated with the goods, goods are pictured and described, and ordering information is provided.

Mark: T.MARKEY YOUR CLOTHING EMPORIUM

Goods: Shirts

• THE MARK IS LOCATED ON THE TOP OF THE WEB PAGE AND IS PROMINENTLY DISPLAYED.

• ALTHOUGH THE MARK IS PLACED ABOVE THE WEBSITE NAVIGATION TABS AND APPEARS IN CONJUNCTION WITH A SLOGAN THAT REFERS TO RETAIL STORE SERVICES (I.E., "YOUR CLOTHING EMPORIUM"), THE MARK STILL APPEARS TO BE ASSOCIATED WITH THE GOODS BECAUSE THE GOODS ARE SHOWN IMMEDIATELY BELOW THE NAVIGATION TABS AND THE IDENTIFIED GOODS ARE THE ONLY PRODUCTS DISPLAYED.

• ANOTHER MARK APPEARS TO BE USED IN CONNECTION WITH THE GOODS (I.E., "LET T.MARKEY BUNDLE YOU UP." AND DESIGN). HOWEVER, MULTIPLE MARKS MAY FUNCTION AS A SOURCE INDICATOR FOR THE SAME GOODS. HERE, BOTH MARKS CONTAIN THE SAME TERM "T.MARKEY," SUGGESTING THE MARKS INDICATE THE SAME SOURCE, AND BOTH ARE PLACED NEAR AND IN ASSOCIATION WITH THE GOODS.

• THE WEB PAGE PROVIDES PRODUCT INFORMATION IN THE FORM OF PICTURES AND DESCRIPTIONS OF THE GOODS, PRICES, AND SIZE OPTIONS.

• THE TELEPHONE NUMBER IS AN ACCEPTABLE MEANS OF ORDERING, EVEN THOUGH IT IS NOT ACCOMPANIED WITH SPECIAL ORDERING INSTRUCTIONS, BECAUSE THERE IS SUFFICIENT PRODUCT INFORMATION TO MAKE THE DECISION TO PURCHASE THE GOODS AND THE TELEPHONE NUMBER IS PROM-INENTLY DISPLAYED AND POSITIONED IN CLOSE PROXIMITY TO THE PRODUCT INFORMATION, IMPLYING THAT THE GOODS MAY BE ORDERED BY CALLING THE TELEPHONE NUMBER. IF THE TELEPHONE NUMBER HAD BEEN LISTED NEAR OR AS PART OF APPLICANT'S ADDRESS, IT WOULD NOT BE SUFFICIENT ORDERING INFORMATION SINCE IT WOULD BE PERCEIVED AS PART OF THE CORPORATE CONTACT INFORMATION AND NOT AS A MEANS FOR PURCHASING THE GOODS.

Association is more likely when the applied-for mark is physically near the goods and no other marks appear to be used in connection with the goods, as in Example 9.

Example 9: Mark is associated with the goods, goods are pictured and described, and ordering information is provided.

Mark: TEEYAK

Goods: Sunglasses and hats

• THE MARK APPEARS BELOW THE WEBSITE NAVIGATION TABS AND IS PROMINENTLY DISPLAYED IN LARGE FONT FOLLOWED BY THE "TM" DESIGNATION.

• THE MARK IS PHYSICALLY CLOSE TO THE GOODS AND IS DIRECTLY ASSOCIATED WITH THEM.

• ALTHOUGH ANOTHER MARK (I.E.,"T.MARKEY YOUR CLOTHING EMPORIUM") APPEARS ON THE WEB PAGE, IT SEEMS TO FUNCTION AS A RETAIL STORE SERVICE MARK SINCE IT IS LOCATED WHERE SERVICE MARKS ARE COMMONLY PLACED, THERE IS OTHER MATTER SEPARATING THE MARK FROM THE GOODS, AND THERE IS ANOTHER MARK PLACED CLOSER TO THE GOODS AND BETTER ASSOCIATED WITH THEM.

• PRODUCT INFORMATION IS PROVIDED IN THE FORM OF PICTURES AND DESCRIPTIONS OF THE GOODS ALONG WITH PRICES.

• THE LINKS UNDER EACH PRODUCT COMBINED WITH THE "BUY ONLINE NOW!" INSTRUCTION INDICATE THAT DIRECT ORDERING IS POSSIBLE.

• IN THE ABSENCE OF LINKS AND THE "BUY ONLINE NOW!" INSTRUCTION, THE TELEPHONE NUMBER WOULD NOT BE ACCEPTABLE ORDERING INFORMATION BECAUSE IT APPEARS TO BE PART OF CORPORATE CONTACT INFORMATION PROVIDED TO OBTAIN INFORMATION ABOUT THE PRODUCT OR THE COMPANY AND NOT INTENDED AS A MEANS OF PLACING OR ACCEPTING ORDERS.

Association becomes less likely if other marks are used in connection with the goods and appear to be trademarks for those goods, as in Example 10.

Example 10: Applied-for mark does not function as a trademark.

Mark: LEADING EDGE TONERS

Goods: Numerous goods including toner, toner cartridges, ink sticks, components for laser toner cartridges, and printer parts

• USE OF THE APPLIED-FOR MARK IN THE URL IDENTIFIES THE WEBSITE WHERE APPLICANT'S RETAIL SERVICES ARE CONDUCTED AND DOES NOT SHOW TRADEMARK USE.

• THE APPLIED-FOR MARK FUNCTIONS AS A SERVICE MARK FOR RETAIL STORE OR DISTRIBUTORSHIP SERVICES, RATHER THAN AS A TRADEMARK, BECAUSE IT APPEARS IN THE UPPER-LEFT CORNER OF THE WEB PAGE WHERE SERVICE MARKS NORMALLY APPEAR AND THERE ARE OTHER MARKS THAT APPEAR TO BE USED IN CONNECTION WITH THE GOODS.

• THE USE OF THE APPLIED-FOR MARK IN PHRASES CONTAINING THIRD-PARTY TRADEMARKS THAT ARE USED TO IDENTIFY GOODS OF THIRD PARTIES (E.G., "LEADING EDGE TONERS BEST PRICES FOR TEKTRONIX TONERS" OR "THE PRICE LEADER FOR XEROX/TEKTRONIX TONER.") DOES NOT CONSTITUTE TRADEMARK USE AND, INSTEAD, SIGNIFIES THAT THE APPLICANT IS A RETAIL STORE OR DISTRIBUTORSHIP THAT SELLS THE GOODS OF OTHERS

904.03(I)(C) ORDERING INFORMATION

A point-of-sale web-page display must provide a means of ordering the goods, either directly from the web page itself (e.g., web page contains a "shop online" button or link) or from information gleaned from the web page (e.g., web page lists a telephone number designated for ordering). *See In re Quantum Foods, Inc.*, 94 USPQ2d 1375, 1378-79 (TTAB 2010); *In re Osterberg*, 83 USPQ2d 1220, 1224 (TTAB 2007) . If the web page offers no way to purchase the goods, the web page is merely an advertisement and not a display associated with the goods. *See In re Quantum Foods, Inc.*, 94 USPQ2d at 1378-80; *In re Osterberg*, 83 USPQ2d at 1224; In re Genitope Corp., 78 USPQ2d 1819, 1822 (TTAB 2006).

Indicators of the ability to buy the goods via the web page may include:

• A SALES ORDER FORM TO PLACE AN ORDER, AN ONLINE PROCESS TO ACCEPT AN ORDER, SUCH AS "SHOPPING CART" FUNCTIONALITY, OR SPECIAL INSTRUCTIONS ON HOW TO ORDER;

• INFORMATION ON MINIMUM QUANTITIES;

• INDICATION OF METHODS OF PAYMENT;

• INFORMATION ABOUT SHIPMENT OF THE GOODS; AND/OR

• MEANS OF CONTACTING THE APPLICANT TO PLACE AN ORDER.

See In re Anpath Grp., 95 USPQ2d 1377, 1381 (TTAB 2010) ; In re Quantum Foods, Inc., 94 USPQ2d at 1379.

Determining the sufficiency of ordering information is a nuanced analysis requiring an examination of the web page content and layout in terms of the level of detail provided about both the goods and the means for ordering them. The more specific and clear the means of immediately and directly ordering the goods on the web page (e.g., "shopping cart" or "Call 1-800-xxx-xxxx to Order Now"), the less detailed the information about the product features and specifications needs to be (e.g., price, size, color, or style), as shown in Example 11.

Example 11: Mark is associated with the goods, goods are pictured and described, and ordering information is provided.

Mark: RING IN THE NEW YEAR WITH OUR RINGS
Goods: Rings
• THE MARK IS PLACED ON THE BOTTOM OF THE WEB PAGE AND IS FOLLOWED BY THE "TM" DESIGNATION.

• THE MARK IS CLOSE TO THE PICTURE OF THE GOODS AND CONTAINS THE TERM "RINGS" WHICH REFERENCES THE GOODS.

• THE "SHOP ONLINE" TAB AND THE "SHOP" LINK INDICATE DIRECT ORDERING VIA THE WEB PAGE.

• WEB PAGE IS ALSO ACCEPTABLE FOR GOODS IF THE PROPOSED MARK WERE "T.MARKEY JEWELRY" (IN UPPER-LEFT CORNER) BECAUSE IT IS LOCATED CLOSE TO THE PICTURE OF THE GOODS AND BOTH THE PROPOSED MARK AND THE "T.MARKEY JEWELRY" MARK INDICATE COMMON ORIGIN SINCE IT CAN BE INFERRED THAT THE WORDING "OUR RINGS" IN THE PROPOSED MARK REFERS TO RINGS BY T.MARKEY JEWELRY.

Conversely, the more detailed the product information is on the web page, the less detailed the ordering information needs to be (e.g., providing a telephone number without specifically stating that it be used to place orders). *See Example 8* at TMEP §904.03(i)(B)(2). Although pricing information is normally associated with ordering goods, the presence or absence of pricing on its own is not determinative of wheter the web page provides sufficient ordering information. *Compare In re Dell Inc.*, 71 USPQ2d 1725, 1728-29 (TTAB 2004) (concluding that a web-page specimen used in connection with applicant's computer hardware, which provided information about the goods but did not show the price of the goods, met the requirements for a display associated with the goods), and TMEP §904.03(h) (indicating that it is not necessary for a catalog specimen to list the price of the goods in order to meet the criteria for a display associated with the goods), with *In re Quantum Foods, Inc.*, 94 USPQ2d at 1379 (listing pricing information as information normally associated with ordering goods and noting the absence of pricing or other ordering information on the applicant's web page specimen to purchase the goods), and *In re MediaShare Corp.*, 43 USPQ2d 1304, 1305 (TTAB 1997) (concluding that applicant's specimen was merely advertising material because it lacked the price of the goods and other information normally associated with ordering goods). If the goods can be ordered via the information contained on the web page, then, presumably, the price will be presented at some point before the order is completed.

See TMEP §§904.03(i)(C)(1)-904.03(i)(C)(3) for a discussion of the common features of websites and the issues to consider when determining whether these features constitute sufficient means of ordering the goods.

904.03(I)   Specimens for Motion Marks

To show that a motion mark actually identifies and distinguishes the goods/services and indicates their source, an applicant must submit a specimen that depicts the motion sufficiently to show how the mark is used on or in connection with the goods/services, and that matches the required description of the mark. Although the drawing for a motion mark may depict a single point in the movement, or up to five freeze frames showing various points in the movement, an acceptable specimen should show the entire repetitive motion in order to depict the commercial impression conveyed by the mark (e.g. , a video clip, a series of still photos, or a series of screen shots).

For TEAS applications under §1(a), as well as response, statement of use/amendment to allege use, petition, and registration maintenance/renewal forms, the specimen can be attached to the TEAS form and must be an electronic file in .wav, .wmv, .wma, .mp3, .mpg, or .avi format. Audio files should not exceed 5 MB in size and video files should not exceed 30 MB because TEAS cannot accommodate larger files.

See TMEP §807.11 regarding drawings for motion marks and TMEP §904.02(a) regarding specimens filed electronically.

TMEP Chapter 1300

Service Marks, Collective Marks and Certification Marks

You are a goods provider if customers purchase physical products
from you that bear your trademark. Like shoes or laptops or candy.

You are a services provider if customers pay you to perform an activity for them.
Like landscaping or accounting or dry cleaning.

See the difference?
Goods are things that bear your trademark.
Services are activities that you perform for others.

If you apply for goods, you may submit a photograph
of the mark on the goods themselves, or on a label or hangtag
that is attached to the goods.
Packaging that shows the mark is also acceptable.
Source: USPTO Video

Chapter 1300 - Service Marks, Collective Marks, and Certification Marks

The Trademark Act of 1946 provides for registration of trademarks, service marks, collective trademarks, and service marks, collective membership marks, and certification marks. 15 U.S.C. §§1051, 1053, and 1054. The language of this Manual is generally directed to trademarks. Procedures for trademarks usually apply to other types of marks, unless otherwise stated. This chapter is devoted to special circumstances relating to service marks, collective marks, collective membership marks, and certification marks.

AUTHOR'S COMMENTS

Certification Marks protect products grown in their "Region of Origin" Agricultural and animal products such as: Brazilian Coffee, Hawaii's Kona Coffee, wines and cheeses from various regions of the world, Georgia's Vidalia Onions, Maui's Sweet Onions and meats from Italy, Argentine, Butter from Hokkaido, Japan and distilled liquor from Tennessee, Canada, Scotland and French Champagne, and the list goes on.
The Certification Marks are generally sponsored by organizations such as: Local Chamber of Commerce, Government Agricultural Departments, Agricultural Universities and Cooperatives.

Example of a Certification Mark

Word Mark: Certified Grown in Idaho
  100% IDAHO POTATOES
Mark Drawing Code: (3) Design Plus Words, Letters, And/Or Numbers
Description of Mark: The color(s) Brown (Dark Areas), White and Gold (Gray Areas) ...
Type of Mark: Certification

The certification mark, as used by authorized persons, certifies the regional origin of potatoes grown in the State of Idaho and certifies that those potatoes conform to grade, size, weight, color, shape, cleanliness, variety, internal defect, external defect, maturity and residue level standards promulgated by the certifier.
(APPLICANT) Idaho Potato Commission STATE AGENCY IDAHO
P.O. Box 1670, 661 South Rivershore Lane, Suite 230, Eagle IDAHO 83616

1301 SERVICE MARKS

Section 45 of the Trademark Act, 15 U.S.C. §1127, defines "service mark" as follows:

The term "service mark" means any word, name, symbol, or device, or any combination thereof--

• (1) USED BY A PERSON, OR

• (2) WHICH A PERSON HAS A BONA FIDE INTENTION TO USE IN COMMERCE AND APPLIES TO REGISTER ON THE PRINCIPAL REGISTER ESTABLISHED BY THIS [ACT],

to identify and distinguish the services of one person, including a unique service, from the services of others and to indicate the source of the services, even if that source is unknown. Titles, character names, and other distinctive features of radio or television programs may be registered as service marks notwithstanding that they, or the programs, may advertise the goods of the sponsor.

Therefore, to be registrable as a service mark, the asserted mark must function both to *identify* the services recited in the application and distinguish them from the services of others, and to *indicate the source* of the recited services, even if that source is unknown. The activities recited in the identification must constitute services as contemplated by the Trademark Act. *See* TMEP §§1301.01 *et seq.*

If a proposed mark does not function as a service mark for the services recited, or if the applicant is not rendering a registrable service, the statutory basis for refusal of registration on the Principal Register is §§1, 2, 3, and 45 of the Trademark Act, 15 U.S.C. §§1051, 1052, 1053, and 1127.

See TMEP §1303 concerning collective service marks.

1301.01 WHAT IS A SERVICE?

A service mark can only be registered for activities that constitute services as contemplated by the Trademark Act. 15 U.S.C. §§1051, 1052, 1053, and 1127. The Trademark Act defines the term "service mark," but it does not define what constitutes a service. Many activities are obviously services (e.g., dry cleaning, banking, shoe repairing, transportation, and house painting).

1301.01(a) Criteria for Determining What Constitutes a Service

The following criteria have evolved for determining what constitutes a service: (1) a service must be a real activity; (2) a service must be performed to the order of, or for the benefit of, someone other than the applicant; and (3) the activity performed must be qualitatively different from anything necessarily done in connection with the sale of the applicant's goods or the performance of another service.

1301.01(a)(i)   Performance of a Real Activity

A service must be a real activity. A mere idea or concept, e.g., an idea for an accounting organizational format or a recipe for a baked item, is not a service. Similarly, a system, process, or method is not a service.   In re Universal Oil Prods. Co., 476 F.2d 653, 177 USPQ 456 (C.C.P.A. 1973); In re Citibank, N.A., 225 USPQ 612 (TTAB 1985); In re Scientific Methods, Inc., 201 USPQ 917 (TTAB 1979); In re McCormick & Co., 179 USPQ 317 (TTAB 1973). See TMEP §1301.02(e) regarding marks that identify a system or process.

The commercial context must be considered in determining whether a real service is being performed. For example, at one time the activities of grocery stores, department stores, and similar retail stores were not considered to be services. However, it has long been recognized that gathering various products together, making a place available for purchasers to select goods, and providing any other necessary means for consummating purchases constitutes the performance of a service.

1301.02   What Is a Service Mark?

Not every word, combination of words, or other designation used in the performance or advertising of services is registrable as a service mark. To function as a service mark, the asserted mark must be used in a way that identifies and distinguishes the source of the services recited in the application. Even if it is clear that the applicant is rendering a service (see TMEP §§1301.01 et seq.), the record must show that the asserted mark actually identifies and distinguishes the source of the service recited in the application. In re Adver. & Mktg. Dev. Inc., 821 F.2d 614, 2 USPQ2d 2010 (Fed. Cir. 1987) (stationery specimen showed use of THE NOW GENERATION as a mark for applicant's advertising or promotional services as well as to identify a licensed advertising campaign, where the recited services were specified in a byline appearing immediately beneath the mark).

The fact that the proposed mark appears in an advertisement or brochure in which the services are advertised does not in itself show use as a mark. The record must show that there is a direct association between the mark and the service. See In re Universal Oil Prods. Co., 476 F.2d 653, 177 USPQ 456 (C.C.P.A. 1973) (term that identifies only a process does not function as a service mark, even where services are advertised in the same specimen brochure in which the name of the process is used); In re Graystone Consulting Assocs., 115 USPQ2d 2035 (TTAB 2015) (finding specimen did not show a direct association between the mark WALK-IN SHOPPER and the identified business training consultancy services, but instead showed the mark being used to identify a particular type of customer that is the focus of the consulting services); In re Duratech Indus. Inc., 13 USPQ2d 2052 (TTAB 1989) (term used on bumper sticker with no reference to the services does not function as a mark); Peopleware Sys., Inc. v. Peopleware, Inc., 226 USPQ 320 (TTAB 1985) (term PEOPLE-WARE used within a byline on calling card specimen does not constitute service mark usage of that term, even if specimen elsewhere shows that applicant provides the recited services); In re J.F. Pritchard & Co., 201 USPQ 951 (TTAB 1979) (proposed mark used only to identify a liquefaction process in brochure advertising the services does not function as a mark, because there is no direct association between the mark and the offering of services). See TMEP §1301.04(b).

The question of whether a designation functions as a mark that identifies and distinguishes the recited services is determined by examining the specimen(s) and any other evidence in the record that shows how the designation is used. In re Morganroth, 208 USPQ 284 (TTAB 1980); In re Republic of Austria Spanische Reitschule, 197 USPQ 494 (TTAB 1977). It is the perception of the ordinary customer that determines whether the asserted mark functions as a service mark, not the applicant's intent, hope, or expectation that it do so. In re Standard Oil Co., 275 F.2d 945, 125 USPQ 227 (C.C.P.A. 1960). Factors that the examining attorney should consider in determining whether the asserted mark functions as a service mark include whether the wording claimed as a mark is physically separate from textual matter, whether a term is displayed in capital letters or enclosed in quotation marks, and the manner in which a term is used in relation to other material on the specimen.

While a service mark does not have to be displayed in any particular size or degree of prominence, it must be used in a way that makes a commercial impression separate and apart from the other elements of the advertising matter or other material upon which it is used, such that the designation will be recognized by prospective purchasers as a source identifier. *In re C.R. Anthony Co., 3 USPQ2d 1894 (TTAB 1987); In re Post Props., Inc., 227 USPQ 334 (TTAB 1985).* The proposed mark must not blend so well with other matter on specimen that it is difficult or impossible to discern what the mark is. *In re McDonald's Corp., 229 USPQ 555 (TTAB 1985) ; In re Royal Viking Line A/S, 216 USPQ 795 (TTAB 1982); In re Republic of Austria Spanische Reitschule, supra; Ex parte Nat'l Geographic Soc'y, 83 USPQ 260 (Comm'r Pats. 1949).*

On the other hand, the fact that the proposed mark is prominently displayed does not in and of itself make it registrable, if it is not used in a manner that would be perceived by consumers as an indicator of source. *In re Wakefern Food Corp., 222 USPQ 76 (TTAB 1984).* The important question is not how readily a mark will be noticed but whether, when noticed, it will be understood as identifying and indicating the origin of the services. *In re Singer Mfg. Co., 255 F.2d 939, 118 USPQ 310 (C.C.P.A. 1958).* The presence of the "SM" symbol is not dispositive of the issue of whether matter sought to be registered is used as a service mark. *In re British Caledonian Airways Ltd., 218 USPQ 737 (TTAB 1983).*

1301.02(a) Matter that Does Not Function as a Service Mark

To function as a service mark, a designation must be used in a manner that would be perceived by purchasers as identifying and distinguishing the source of the services recited in the application. *See In re Keep A Breast Found., 123 USPQ2d 1869, 1882 (TTAB 2017)* (finding that three-dimensional cast of female breast and torso would be perceived as something that applicant assists in making as part of applicant's associational and educational services, rather than as a mark designating the source of the services).

Use of a designation or slogan to convey advertising or promotional information, rather than to identify and indicate the source of the services, is not service mark use. See *In re Standard Oil Co., 275 F.2d 945, 125 USPQ 227 (C.C.P.A. 1960)* (GUARANTEED STARTING found to be ordinary words that convey information about the services, not a service mark for the services of "winterizing" motor vehicles); *In re Melville Corp., 228 USPQ 970 (TTAB 1986)* (BRAND NAMES FOR LESS found to be informational phrase that does not function as a mark for retail store services); *In re Brock Residence Inns, Inc., 222 USPQ 920 (TTAB 1984)* (FOR A DAY, A WEEK, A MONTH OR MORE so highly descriptive and informational in nature that purchasers would be unlikely to perceive it as an indicator of the source of hotel services); *In re Wakefern Food Corp., 222 USPQ 76 (TTAB 1984)* (WHY PAY MORE found to be a common commercial phrase that does not serve to identify grocery store services); *In re Gilbert Eiseman, P.C., 220 USPQ 89 (TTAB 1983)* (IN ONE DAY not used as source identifier but merely as a component of advertising matter that conveyed a characteristic of applicant's plastic surgery services); *In re European-American Bank & Trust Co., 201 USPQ 788 (TTAB 1979)* (slogan THINK ABOUT IT found to be an informational or instructional phrase that would not be perceived as a mark for banking services); *In re Restonic Corp., 189 USPQ 248 (TTAB 1975)* (phrase used merely to advertise goods manufactured and sold by applicant's franchisees does not serve to identify franchising services). *Cf. In re Post Props., Inc., 227 USPQ 334 (TTAB 1985)* (finding QUALITY SHOWS, set off from text of advertising copy in extremely large typeface and reiterated at the conclusion of the narrative portion of the ad, to be a registrable service mark for applicant's real estate management and leasing services, because it was used in a way that made a commercial impression separate from that of the other elements of advertising material upon which it was used, such that the designation would be recognized by prospective customers as a source identifier). See TMEP §1202.04 regarding informational matter that does not function as a trademark.

A term that is used only to identify a product, device, or instrument sold or used in the performance of a service rather than to identify the service itself does not function as a service mark. *See In re Moody's Investors Serv. Inc., 13 USPQ2d 2043 (TTAB 1989)* ("Aaa," as used on the specimen, found to identify the applicant's ratings instead of its rating services); *In re Niagara Frontier Servs., Inc., 221 USPQ 284 (TTAB 1983)* (WE MAKE IT, YOU BAKE IT only identifies pizza, and does not function as a service mark to identify grocery store services); In re British Caledonian Airways Ltd., 218 USPQ 737 (TTAB 1983) (term that identifies a seat in the first-class section of an airplane does not function as mark for air transportation services); *In re Editel Prods., Inc., 189 USPQ 111 (TTAB 1975)* (MINI-MOBILE identifies only a vehicle used in rendering services and does not serve to identify the production of television videotapes for others); *In re Oscar Mayer & Co., 171 USPQ 571 (TTAB 1971)* (WIENERMOBILE does not function as mark for advertising and promoting the sale of wieners, where it is used only to identify a vehicle used in rendering claimed services).

Similarly, a term that only identifies a process, style, method, or system used in rendering the services is not registrable as a service mark, unless it is also used to identify and distinguish the service. See TMEP §1301.02(e).

A term that only identifies a menu item does not function as a mark for restaurant services. *In re El Torito Rest. Inc., 9 USPQ2d 2002 (TTAB 1988).*

The name or design of a character or person does not function as a service mark, unless it identifies and distinguishes the services in addition to identifying the character or person. See TMEP §1301.02(b).

A term used only as a trade name is not registrable as a service mark. *See In re The Signal Cos., 228 USPQ 956 (TTAB 1986)* (journal advertisement submitted as specimen showed use of ONE OF THE SIGNAL COMPANIES merely as an informational slogan, where words appeared only in small, subdued typeface underneath the address and telephone number of applicant's subsidiary). See TMEP §1202.01 for additional information about matter used solely as a trade name.

If a service mark would be perceived only as decoration or ornamentation when used in connection with the identified services, it must be refused as nondistinctive trade dress under Trademark Act §§1, 2, 3, and 45, 15 U.S.C. §§1051-1052, 1127. Matter that is merely ornamental in nature does not function as a service mark. *See In re Tad's Wholesale, Inc., 132 USPQ 648 (TTAB 1962) (wallpaper design not registrable as a service mark for restaurant services).* See TMEP §1202.02(b)–1202.02(b)(ii) regarding trade dress.

See TMEP §1202.02(a)(vii) regarding functionality and service marks.

1301.02(b) Names of Characters or Personal Names as Service Marks

Under 15 U.S.C. §1127, a name or design of a character does not function as a service mark, unless it identifies and distinguishes services in addition to identifying the character. If the name or design is used only to identify the character, it is not registrable as a service mark. *In re Hechinger Inv. Co. of Del., 24 USPQ2d 1053 (TTAB 1991)* (design of dog appearing in advertisement does not function as mark for retail hardware and housewares services); *In re McDonald's Corp., 229 USPQ 555 (TTAB 1985)* (APPLE PIE TREE does not function as mark for restaurant services, where the specimen shows use of mark only to identify one character in a procession of characters); *In re Whataburger Sys., Inc., 209 USPQ 429 (TTAB 1980)* (design of zoo animal character distributed to restaurant customers in the form of an iron-on patch not used in a manner that would be perceived as an indicator of source); *In re Burger King Corp., 183 USPQ 698 (TTAB 1974)* (fanciful design of king does not serve to identify and distinguish restaurant services). See TMEP §1202.10 regarding the registrability of the names and designs of characters in creative works.

Similarly, personal names (actual names and pseudonyms) of individuals or groups function as marks only if they identify and distinguish the services recited and not merely the individual or group. *In re Mancino, 219 USPQ 1047 (TTAB 1983)* (holding that BOOM BOOM would be viewed by the public solely as applicant's professional boxing nickname and not as an identifier of the service of conducting professional boxing exhibitions); In re Lee Trevino Enters., 182 USPQ 253 (TTAB 1974) (LEE TREVINO used merely to identify a famous professional golfer rather than as a mark to identify and distinguish any services rendered by him); *In re Generation Gap Prods., Inc., 170 USPQ 423 (TTAB 1971)* (GORDON ROSE used only to identify a particular individual and not as a service mark to identify the services of a singing group).

The name of a character or person is registrable as a service mark if the record shows that it is used in a manner that would be perceived by purchasers as identifying the services in addition to the character or person. *In re Fla. Cypress Gardens Inc., 208 USPQ 288 (TTAB 1980)* (name CORKY THE CLOWN used on handbills found to function as a mark to identify live performances by a clown, where the mark was used to identify not just the character but also the act or entertainment service performed by the character); *In re Carson, 197 USPQ 554 (TTAB 1977)* (individual's name held to function as mark, where specimen showed use of the name in conjunction with a reference to services and information as to the location and times of performances, costs of tickets, and places where tickets could be purchased); *In re Ames, 160 USPQ 214 (TTAB 1968)* (name of musical group functions as mark, where name was used on advertisements that prominently featured a photograph of the group and gave the name, address, and telephone number of the group's booking agent); *In re Folk, 160 USPQ 213 (TTAB 1968)* (THE LOLLIPOP PRINCESS functions as a service mark for entertainment services, namely, telling children's stories by radio broadcasting and personal appearances).

See TMEP §§1202.09(a) et seq. regarding the registrability of the names and pseudonyms of authors and performing artists, and TMEP §1202.09(b) regarding the registrability of the names of artists used on original works of art.

1301.02(c)   Three-Dimensional Service Marks

The three-dimensional configuration of a building is registrable as a service mark only if it is used in such a way that it is or could be perceived as a mark. Evidence of use might include menus or letterhead that show promotion of the building's design, or configuration, as a mark. See In re Lean-To Barbecue, Inc., 172 USPQ 151 (TTAB 1971); In re Master Kleens of Am., Inc., 171 USPQ 438 (TTAB 1971) ; In re Griffs of Am., Inc., 157 USPQ 592 (TTAB 1968) . Cf. Fotomat Corp. v. Cochran, 437 F. Supp. 1231, 194 USPQ 128 (D. Kan. 1977); Fotomat Corp. v. Photo Drive-Thru, Inc., 425 F. Supp. 693, 193 USPQ 342 (D.N.J. 1977).

A three-dimensional costume design may function as a mark for entertainment services. *See In re Red Robin Enters., 222 USPQ 911 (TTAB 1984).*

However, the Board has found that a mark consisting of a three-dimensional cylindrical cast of female breasts and torso did not function as a mark for applicant's association, charitable fundraising, and educational services in the field of breast cancer. In re Keep A Breast Found., 123 USPQ2d 1869, 1880 (TTAB 2017). The evidence indicated that the mark was being used as part of applicant's services to assist women to make such casts. Thus, the cast would be perceived as part of the services, rather than as a mark designating the source of the services. Id.

Generally, a photograph is a proper specimen of use for a three-dimensional mark. However, photographs of a building are not sufficient to show use of the building design as a mark for services performed in the building if they only show the building in which the services are performed. The specimen must show that the proposed mark is used in a way that would be perceived as a mark.

See 37 C.F.R. §2.52(b)(2) and TMEP §807.10 regarding drawings of three-dimensional marks.

When examining a three-dimensional mark, the examining attorney must determine whether the proposed mark is inherently distinctive. See TMEP §1202.02(b)(ii).

1301.02(d)   Titles of Radio and Television Programs

The title of a continuing series of presentations (e.g., a television or movie "series," a series of live performances, or a continuing radio program), may constitute a mark for either entertainment services or educational services. However, the title of a single creative work, that is, the title of one episode or event presented as one program, does not function as a service mark. *In re Posthuma, 45 USPQ2d 2011 (TTAB 1998) (term that identifies title of a play not registrable as service mark for entertainment services).* The record must show that the matter sought to be registered is more than the title of one presentation, performance, or recording. See TMEP §§1202.08 et seq. and cases cited therein for further information regarding the registrability of the title of a single creative work.

Specimens that show use of a service mark in relation to television programs or a movie series may be in the nature of a photograph of the video or film frame when the mark is used in the program.

Service marks in the nature of titles of entertainment programs may be owned by the producer of the show, by the broadcasting system or station, or by the author or creator of the show, depending upon the circumstances. Normally, an applicant's statement that the applicant owns the mark is sufficient; the examining attorney should not inquire about ownership, unless information in the record clearly contradicts the applicant's verified statement that it is the owner of the mark.

1301.04(f) Elements of an Acceptable Service-Mark Specimen

To be acceptable, a service-mark specimen must show the mark sought to be registered used in a manner that demonstrates a direct association between the mark and the services. Essentially, the mark must be shown "in a manner that would be perceived by potential purchasers as identifying the applicant's services and indicating their source." *In re DSM Pharm., Inc.*, 87 USPQ2d 1623, 1624 (TTAB 2008) ; see In re JobDiva, Inc.,843 F.3d 936, 941, 121 USPQ2d 1122, 1126 (Fed. Cir.2016) ("To determine whether a mark is used in connection with the services . . . a key consideration is the perception of the user."); *In re Ancor Holdings, LLC,79 USPQ2d 1218, 1220 (TTAB 2006) (citing In re Walker Research, Inc., 228 USPQ 691, 692 (TTAB 1986)).*

The acceptability of a specimen is determined based on the facts and evidence of record, and viewed in the context of the relevant commercial environment. *See In re Ancor Holdings, LLC, 79 USPQ2d at 1220* ("[W]e must base our determination of public perception of applicant's mark on the manner of use of [the mark] in the advertising which has been submitted as a specimen. Further, we must make that determination within the current commercial context, and, in doing so, we may consider any other evidence of record 'bearing on the question of what impact applicant's use is likely to have on purchasers and potential purchasers.'" (quoting *in re Safariland Hunting Corp., 24 USPQ2d 1380, 1381 (TTAB 1992)).* Thus, the information provided by the specimen itself, any explanations offered by the applicant clarifying the nature, content, or context of use of the specimen, and any other information in the record should be considered in the analysis. *In re DSM Pharm., Inc., 87 USPQ2d at 1626* ("In determining whether a specimen is acceptable evidence of service mark use, we may consider applicant's explanations as to how the specimen is used, along with any other available evidence in the record that shows how the mark is actually used."); *In re Ancor Holdings, LLC, 79 USPQ2d at 1220.*

When the identified services involve newer technology, the examining attorney must follow the appropriate examination policies and procedures, but also should employ a practical approach in analyzing the submitted specimen. *See In re Ralph Mantia Inc., 54 USPQ2d 1284, 1286 (TTAB 2000)* (finding a business card and stationery displaying the mark and the word "design" were acceptable specimens of use for applicant's mark in connection with commercial art design services, noting that "[i]t is not necessary that the specific field of design, i.e., commercial art, also appear thereon" and that "the word 'design' alone is sufficient to create in the minds of purchasers an association between the mark and applicant's commercial art services"); *In re Metriplex, Inc., 23 USPQ2d 1315, 1316 (TTAB 1992)* (finding the submitted specimens acceptable to show use of applicant's mark in connection with data transmission services because the specimens showed "the mark as it appears on a computer terminal in the course of applicant's rendering of the service" and noting that "purchasers and users of the service would recognize [applicant's mark], as it appears on the computer screen specimens, as a mark identifying the data transmission services which are accessed via the computer terminal"). This may entail reviewing all the information of record to understand both how the mark is used and how it will be perceived by consumers. *See In re JobDiva*, 121 USPQ2d at 1126; *In re Ancor Holdings, LLC*, 79 USPQ2d at 1221. Additionally, if the examining attorney elects to conduct research regarding the mark, the services, or practices in the particular industry, it may be helpful to consider any information uncovered regarding how the applicant and others in the industry typically advertise and render the identified services in the relevant marketplace, as well as the manner in which service marks are normally used in connection with those services. See TMEP §1301.04(h)(iii) for a discussion of issues surrounding technology-related services.

1301.04(h)(iv)(C) Webpages

Webpages from an applicant's or a third-party's website may be submitted as advertising. This type of specimen is acceptable if it shows the mark used in advertising the identified services and creates the required direct association by referring to the services and by showing the mark being used to identify and distinguish the services and their source. *In re Florists' Transworld Delivery, Inc.*, 119 USPQ2d 1056, 1062 (TTAB 2016).

Webpages lacking a reference to the services may be acceptable if they show use of the mark in rendering the services. *See* TMEP §1301.04(i), Example 14 (OUTERNAUTS). Webpages from social-networking websites should be scrutinized to ensure that the mark is properly associated with the identified services. Some applicants may mistakenly mischaracterize their services as "social networking" because they assume that advertising or promoting their non-social-networking services via a social-networking website means they are providing social-networking services. For instance, an applicant may mistakenly file an application for "online social-networking services" and provide a Facebook® webpage as a specimen when, in fact, they operate a pet store and are only using the Facebook® website to advertise the pet store and communicate information to and messages with actual and potential customers. Such a specimen is not acceptable for the social-networking services since it does not demonstrate that the applicant is providing these services. See In re Florists' Transworld Delivery, Inc., 119 USPQ2d at 1057 ("[A]n applicant generally will not be able to rely on use of its social media account to support an application for registration of a mark for [the service of creating an online community for users].").

1301.04(h)(iv)(D) Software Applications ("Apps")

Software applications ("apps") for smartphones and computer tablets are now commonly used to provide online services. Apps are simply the interface that enables the providers of the services to reach the users and render the services, and the users to access those services. Common specimens for such apps are usually screenshots of electronic devices showing the apps rendering the services. Such a specimen will not always depict proper service-mark use of the mark in connection with the identified services unless the displayed screenshot clearly and legibly shows the mark associated with the identified services as the services are rendered or performed via the app. Mere depiction of the mark in the screenshot without sufficient depiction of the activity identified in the services does not establish service mark use within the definition of "use in commerce" under Trademark Act Section 45. 15 U.S.C §1127 ("For purposes of this chapter, a mark shall be deemed to be in use in commerce – (2) on services when it is used or displayed in the sale or advertising of services and the services are rendered in commerce[.]") *See TMEP §1301.04(i), Example 15 (KURBKARMA).*

1302 Collective Marks Generally

Section 45 of the Trademark Act, 15 U.S.C. §1127, defines "collective mark" as follows: The term "collective mark" means a trademark or service mark--

• (1) used by the members of a cooperative, an association, or other collective group or organization, or

• (2) which such cooperative, association, or other collective group or organization has a bona fide intention to use in commerce and applies to register on the principal register established by this [Act], and includes marks indicating membership in a union, an association, or other organization.

Under the Trademark Act, a collective mark is owned by a collective entity even though the mark is used by the members of the collective.

There are basically **two types of collective marks: (1) collective trademarks or collective service marks;** and (2) **collective membership marks.** The distinction between these types of collective marks is explained in *Aloe Creme Labs., Inc. v. Am. Soc'y for Aesthetic Plastic Surgery, Inc.,* 192 USPQ 170, 173 (TTAB 1976), as follows:

A **collective trademark or collective service mark** is a mark adopted by a "collective" (i.e., an association, union, cooperative, fraternal organization, or other organized collective group) for use only by its members, who in turn use the mark to identify their goods or services and distinguish them from those of nonmembers. The "collective" itself neither sells goods nor performs services under a collective trademark or collective service mark, but the collective may advertise or otherwise promote the goods or services sold or rendered by its members under the mark. A **collective membership mark** is a mark adopted for the purpose of indicating membership in an organized collective group, such as a union, an association, or other organization. Neither the collective nor its members uses the collective member-ship mark to identify and distinguish goods or services; rather, the sole function of such a mark is to indicate that the person displaying the mark is a member of the organized collective group.

See also In re Int'l Inst. of Valuers, 223 USPQ 350 (TTAB 1984) . See TMEP §1303 concerning collective trademarks and service marks; TMEP §1304 concerning collective membership marks; and TMEP §1305 concerning the distinction between collective trademarks or service marks from trademarks and service marks used by collective organizations.

1303 Collective Trademarks and Collective Service Marks Generally

Although collective trademarks and collective service marks indicate the commercial origin of goods or services, they also indicate that the party providing the goods or services is a member of a certain group and meets the group's standards for admission. A collective mark is used by all members of the collective group; therefore, no one member can own the mark, and the collective organization holds the title to the collectively used mark for the benefit of all members of the group. In comparison, a trademark or service mark is used by the owner of the mark to indicate the commercial source or origin of the goods/services in the owner.

The collective organization itself neither sells the goods nor renders the services provided under the mark, but may advertise so as to publicize the mark and promote the goods or services sold by its members under the mark. For example, a collective organization of real-estate professionals does not render real-estate services, but rather promotes the real-estate services offered by its members. *See Zimmerman v. Nat'l Assoc. of Realtors,* 70 USPQ2d 1425, 1428 (TTAB 2004).

Compared with a specimen for a trademark or service mark, which generally shows use of the mark by the owner, a specimen of use for a collective trademark or collective service mark must show use of the mark by a member of the collective organization. 37 C.F.R. §2.44(a)(4)(i)(C); TMEP §1303.01(a)(i)(C). Such use must be on the member's goods/packaging or in the sale, advertising, or rendering of the member's services. See37 C.F.R. §2.56(b)(3); TMEP §1303.01(a)(i)(C).

1303.01(a) Filing Basis

All applications for registration must include a filing basis, regardless of the type of mark, because this is the statutory basis for filing an application for registration of a mark in the United States. TMEP §806. There are five filing bases: (1) use of a mark in commerce under §1(a) of the Act; (2) bona fide intention to use a mark in commerce under §1(b) of the Act; (3) a claim of priority, based on an earlier-filed foreign application under §44(d) of the Act; (4) ownership of a registration of the mark in the applicant's country of origin under §44(e) of the Act; and (5) extension of protection of an international registration to the United States under §66(a) of the Act. 15 U.S.C. §§1051(a)-(b), 1126(d)-(e), 1141f(a); 37 C.F.R. §2.44(a)(4).

An applicant is not required to specify or otherwise satisfy the requirements for a filing basis to receive a filing date. SeeKraft Grp. LLC v. Harpole, 90 USPQ2d 1837, 1840 (TTAB 2009). If a §1 or §44 application does not specify a basis, the examining attorney must require in the first Office action that the applicant specify the basis for filing and submit all the elements required for that basis. If the applicant timely responds to the first Office action, but fails to specify a basis for filing, or fails to submit all the elements required for a particular basis, the examining attorney will issue a final Office action, if the application is otherwise in condition for final action.

In a §66(a) application, the basis for filing will have been established in the international registration on file at the IB.

See 37 C.F.R. §2.44(a)(4) and TMEP §1301(a)(i)-(v) for a list of the requirements for each basis.

1304.01 Collective Membership Marks Generally

The sole purpose of a collective membership mark is to indicate that the user of the mark is a member of a particular organization. *See Constitution Party of Tex. v. Constitution Ass'n USA, 152 USPQ 443* (TTAB 1966) (holding cancellation of collective membership mark registration proper since mark was not being used to indicate membership in registrant).

Thus, membership marks are not trademarks or service marks in the ordinary sense; they are not used in business or trade, and they do not indicate commercial origin of goods or services. Registration of these marks fills the need of collective organizations who do not use the symbols of their organizations on goods or services but who still wish to protect their marks from use by others. *See Ex parte Supreme Shrine of the Order of the White Shrine of Jerusalem,* 109 USPQ 248 (Comm'r Pats. 1956), regarding the rationale for registration of collective membership marks.

A collective membership mark may comprise an individual letter or combination of letters, a single word or combination of words, a design alone, a name or nickname, or other matter that identifies the collective organization or indicates its purpose. A membership mark may, but need not, include the term "member" or the equivalent.

In addition to the mark being printed (the most common form), a membership mark may consist of an object, such as a flag, or may be a part of articles of jewelry, such as lapel pins or rings. See TMEP §§1304.02(a)(i) and 1304.02(a)(i)(C) regarding use of membership marks and acceptable specimens.

Nothing in the Trademark Act prohibits the use of the same mark as a membership mark by members and, also, as a trademark or a service mark by the parent organization, but the same mark may not be used both as a membership mark and as a certification mark. 37 C.F.R. §2.45(f); TMEP §1306.04(f).

See TMEP §1302.01 regarding the history of collective membership marks.

1306 Certification Marks

1306.01 Types of Certification Marks

Section 4 of the Trademark Act, provides for the registration of "certification marks, including indications of regional origin," which are defined in Section 45 as follows:

The term "certification mark" means any word, name, symbol, or device, or any combination thereof--

• (1) used by a person other than its owner, or

• (2) which its owner has a bona fide intention to permit a person other than the owner to use in commerce and files an application to register on the principal register established by this [Act],

to certify regional or other origin, material, mode of manufacture, quality, accuracy, or other characteristics of such person's goods or services or that the work or labor on the goods or services was performed by members of a union or other organization.

1306.05(g)(ii) Considerations When the Proposed Mark Contains a Geographic Designation but Is Not a Geographic Certification Mark

When the application is for a mark that contains a geographic designation but is not a geographic certification mark, the examining attorney should consider citing not only any prior mark with distinctive elements (e.g., suggestive, arbitrary, or fanciful wording, or distinctive design elements) that are confusingly similar to those in the applied-for mark, but also any prior geographic certification mark containing a geographic designation that is confusingly similar to the geographic designation in the applied-for mark. Even if the geographic designation in the applied-for mark is not the dominant element, is relatively inconspicuous, or appears with a number of other elements, it may nonetheless be appropriate to cite a prior geographic certification mark that contains the same designation. By contrast, if there are no prior geographic certification marks containing the geographic designation, but there are numerous prior trademarks or service marks that contain and disclaim the designation, then a §2(d) refusal based on the fact that the respective marks share the designation is likely not appropriate.

1306.05(h) American Viticultural Areas

American Viticultural Areas (AVA) are defined grape-growing regions in the United States, created on petition by interested parties through the federal rulemaking process. AVA designations appear on wine labels and "allow vintners and consumers to attribute a given quality, reputation, or other characteristic of a wine made from grapes grown in an area to its geographic origin." Thus, these designations facilitate the accurate description of wine origins and aid consumers in identifying wines. See U.S. Dept. of the Treasury, Alcohol and Tobacco Tax and Trade Bureau, *American Viticultural Area (AVA)*, https://www.ttb.gov/wine/ava.shtml (accessed June 30, 2014). The currently recognized AVA designations can be found at 27 C.F.R. Part 9, Subpart C. In addition, the Alcohol and Tobacco Tax and Trade Bureau of the U.S. Department of the Treasury provides an up-to-date alphabetical list of the designations at https://www.ttb.gov/wine/us_by_ava.shtml.

Although AVA designations are similar to geographic certification marks in terms of their purpose and function, these designations raise complex issues when included in applied-for marks of any type. Thus, if an applied-for mark of any type contains an AVA designation, the assigned examining attorney must consult the Administrator for Trademark Policy and Procedure before taking any action on the application.

Comments from E-trademarks Attorneys

Question:

Can anyone provide insight into the current phenomenon of sophisticated companies with registered marks not using the trademark symbol? This seems to be particularly prevalent on the home pages of some CPG companies as well as new publications. Is this a matter of design strategy? Thank you

Diana Palchik via E-trademarks

Response:

In the wine sector, some label designers and wineries think that the circle R symbol makes the packaging look "too corporate." The theory is that they want to be perceived as family farms and vineyards.

Paul Reidl via E-trademarks

Graphic Designs of Wine Labels are one of the hot areas for the past 20-years. The main theme is to catch your eye on shelves that contain literally hundreds of bottles of wine. The label design may represent the winemaker, geographic location, brand and etc. The logo design may also represent a political wine lobby organization.

This particular wine label is in the "wraparound" category where the label wraps around the bottle, other labels are done in two separate pieces where generally the rear label contains the legal requirements of whichever governing party requires. The thing that interested me about this label is the creative way the designer used the product bar code and blended it into the hills, at the back of the bottle.

Being one of the world's top wine producers, South Africa is a very competitive market for the fruits of the vine. Helderberg Wijnmakerij, therefore, understands the importance of fresh and edgy branding and packaging to help establish a unique identity.

Fanakalo Visual Communication Studio in Stellenbosch took to task and came up with a wraparound label that serves its purpose well. The label had to be visually striking, as well as tactile. This was achieved by illustrating the mountain to look like a lino-cut design rather than the conventional way of etching mountains in a design. Fanakalo extended this look by embossing the clouds above the mountain and making the *barcode on the side of the label work as part of the design.*

The final design manages to be well-balanced, appearing to be just black and white from afar. Closer inspection reveals that every square centimeter of the label has been covered by design. Source: Fanakalo Communication Studio

106

TMEP Chapter 1400

Classification and Identification
of Goods, Services and
Local, U.S. and Global Trademark Search

Chapter 1400 - Classification and Identification of Goods and Services

1401   Classification

1401.01   Statutory Authority

Section 30 of the Trademark Act, 15 U.S.C. §1112, provides authority for establishing a classification system. That section states, in part, as follows:

The Director may establish a classification of goods and services, for convenience of Patent and Trademark Office administration, but not to limit or extend the applicant's or registrant's rights.

1401.02   International Trademark Classification Adopted

As of September 1, 1973, the international classification of goods and services is the controlling classification used by the United States, and it applies to all applications filed on or after September 1, 1973, and their resulting registrations, for all statutory purposes.   See 37 C.F.R. §2.85(a). Unless otherwise indicated, **references in this manual to class refer to the international class.**

Get ready to search - classification and design search codes

Searching the Trademark Electronic Search System (TESS) is an important part of doing a thorough clearance search. Because the TESS database has records for millions of trademarks, you need a strategic approach to search effectively. Design search codes and classes can help you target your search, making it easier to find any trademarks that are likely to cause confusion with yours.

This page will help you identify classes and design search codes to use in your TESS search.

• **Classification of your goods and services** - find out how the USPTO classifies your goods and services to help you narrow your search to trademarks that are used with related goods and services.

• **Design search codes** - if you plan to include a design or logo in your trademark or use any words that could be represented by an image, design search codes allow you to search for trademarks with similar design elements.

Source: USPTO

Develop an effective search

An effective search is:
• Broad enough to find all the trademarks that are likely to cause confusion with yours
• Narrow enough to limit the results you must evaluate to a manageable number of trademarks

If you receive an unmanageably large number of results, you can narrow your search to only the trademarks that are most relevant. A number of tools can help you narrow your search. This page will help you learn to use some of these tools.

Narrow your search conservatively

Narrow your search just enough to limit your results to a number that you can reasonably evaluate. The more you narrow your search, the greater your odds of missing a conflicting trademark in your clearance search.

Being conservative when narrowing your search is crucial. When we examine your application, we will look for trademarks that are likely to cause confusion with your trademark. If we find any, we will not register your trademark, and we can't refund your filing fee.

Classification – find trademarks used on goods and services related to yours

Classification is similar to the departments in a store. Stores categorize merchandise into departments to help you find the products you are looking for, like women's clothing, household appliances, or bed linen. Similarly, classification is a way to categorize goods and services to help you search TESS for goods and services that are similar or related to yours.

There are 45 classes, or categories, that cover all goods and services. Classes 1-34 are for goods, classes 35-45 are for services. Each class can cover a wide range of goods or services. For example, class 25 covers clothing and class 36 covers all insurance and financial services.

Source: USPTO

International Trademark Searching

Nice Agreement archives - general remarks, Class headings and explanatory notes International trademark classification, and the headings of the international trademark classes, are established by the Committee of Experts of the Nice Union and set forth in the International Classification of Goods and Services for the Purposes of the Registration of Marks (Nice Classification), published by the World Intellectual Property Organization ("WIPO"). Click on the links below to view archived versions of the 11th and 10th Edition of the Nice Classification and information regarding changes under 7th and 8th Editions. All editions and versions of the Nice Classification are available on the WIPO website

Global Brand Database

Perform a trademark search by text or image in brand data from multiple national and international sources, including trademarks, appellations of origin and official emblems. V: 2020-02-10 10:4

Search your local area

If you have or expect to have a business, trade name or trademark in your local area it is easy to do an Internet search. I have listed below the two States I have worked in, for example:

State of Ohio
Business name, trade name, trademark search
Entrepreneurs can use the Ohio Secretary of State's business search to search for available business names.

State of Hawaii

The Business Registration Division is a division of the Department of Commerce and Consumer Affairs, a government agency of the State of Hawaii. The Business Registration Branch maintains the business registry for all corporations, limited liability companies, general partnerships, limited partnerships, limited liability partnerships and limited liability limited partnerships conducting business activities in the State. In addition, the registry contains trade names, trademarks, service marks and publicity name rights.

Overview of each international class

This list shows what each class generally covers.
Use the USPTO's Trademark ID Manual to determine which class
or classes cover your goods and services

Goods

001 Chemicals

002 Paints

003 Cosmetics and cleaning products

004 Lubricants and fuels

005 Pharmaceuticals

006 Metal goods

007 Machinery

008 Hand tools

009 Electrical and scientific apparatus

010 Medical apparatus

011 Environmental control apparatus

012 Vehicles

013 Firearms

014 Jewelry

015 Musical instruments

016 Paper goods and printed matter

017 Rubber goods

018 Leather goods

019 Non-metallic building materials

020 Furniture and articles not otherwise

021 Housewares and glass

022 Cordage and fibers

023 Yarns and threads

024 Fabrics

025 Clothing

026 Fancy goods

027 Floor coverings

028 Toys and sporting goods

029 Meats and processed foods

030 Staple foods

031 Natural agricultural products

032 Light beverages

033 Wines and spirits

034 Smokers articles

Services

035 Advertising and business

036 Insurance and financial

037 Construction and repair

038 Communication

039 Transportation and storage

040 Material treatment

041 Education and entertainment

042 Computer, scientific and legal

043 Hotels and restaurants

044 Medical, beauty and agricultural

045 Personal

There are 45 classes, or categories, that cover all goods and services. Classes 1-34 are for goods, classes 35-45 are for services. Each class can cover a wide range of goods or services. Studio 94 Publishing is in Class 41 sub-class 410024 Publication of books.

TMEP Chapter 1900

Madrid Protocol
(Drawing Rules and Specimens)
See Chapter 4 for WIPO Madrid Rules

TMEP Chapter 1900 - Madrid Protocol
(See Chapter 4 of this book for WIPO Madrid Trademark Rules)

The Protocol Relating to the Madrid Agreement Concerning the International Registration of Marks ("Madrid Protocol") is an international treaty that allows a trademark owner to seek registration in any of the countries or intergovernmental organizations that have joined the Madrid Protocol by submitting a single application, called an international application. The international registration system is administered by the International Bureau ("IB") of the World Intellectual Property Organization ("WIPO"), in Geneva, Switzerland.

The Madrid Protocol became effective in the United States on November 2, 2003. The Madrid Protocol Implementation Act of 2002, Pub. L. 107-273, 116 Stat. 1758, 1913-1921 ("MPIA") amended the Trademark Act to provide that: (1) the owner of a United States application and/or registration may seek protection of its mark in any of the countries or intergovernmental organizations party to the Madrid Protocol by submitting a single international application to the IB through the United States Patent and Trademark Office ("USPTO"); and (2) the holder of an international registration may request an extension of protection of the international registration to the United States. A notice of final rulemaking amending the Trademark Rules of Practice to incorporate the MPIA was published at 68 Fed. Reg. 55748 (Sept. 26, 2003).

The Madrid Protocol, *Common Regulations Under the Madrid Agreement Concerning the International Registration of Marks and the Protocol Relating to That Agreement* ("Common Regs."), *Guide to the International Registration of Marks under the Madrid Agreement and the Madrid Protocol* ("Guide to International Registration"), *Administrative Instructions for the Application of the Madrid Agreement Concerning the International Registration of Marks and the Protocol Relating Thereto* ("Admin. Instrs.") are available on the IB's website, at http://www.wipo.int/madrid/en/. The Common Regs. are the procedures agreed to by the parties to the Madrid Protocol regarding the administration of the Madrid Protocol, pursuant to Madrid Protocol Article ("Article") 10(2)(iii).

References below to the Common Regs.,
Guide to the International Registration, and Admin.
Instrs. refer to the September 2009 editions.

1901   Overview of the Madrid System of International Registration

The Madrid system of international registration is governed by two treaties: the Madrid Agreement Concerning the International Registration of Marks, which dates from 1891, and the Protocol Relating to the Madrid Agreement, which was adopted in 1989, entered into force on December 1, 1995, and came into operation on April 1, 1996. The United States is party only to the Protocol, not to the Agreement.

The Madrid system is administered by the IB. To apply for an international registration under the Madrid Protocol, an applicant must be a national of, be domiciled in, or have a real and effective industrial or commercial establishment in one of the countries or intergovernmental organizations that are members of the Protocol ("Contracting Parties"). The application must be based on one or more trademark application(s) filed in, or registration(s) issued by, the trademark office of one of the Contracting Parties ("basic application(s)" or "basic registration(s)"). The international application must be for the same mark and include a list of goods/services that is identical to or narrower than the list of goods/services in the basic application and/or registration. The international application must designate one or more Contracting Parties in which an extension of protection of the international registration is sought.

The applicant must submit the international application through the trademark office of the Contracting Party in which the basic application and/or registration is held ("Office of Origin"). The Office of Origin must certify that the information in the international application corresponds with the information in the basic application and/or registration, and then forward the international application to the IB. If the IB receives the international application within two months of the date of receipt in the Office of Origin, the date of the international registration is the date of receipt in the Office of Origin. If the IB does not receive the international application within two months of the date it was received by the Office of Origin, the date of the international registration is the date on which the international application is received by the IB. See TMEP §1902.04 for information regarding filing requirements that may affect the international registration date.

The international registration is dependent on the basic application and/or registration for five years from the international registration date. If the basic application and/or registration is abandoned, cancelled, or expired, in whole or in part, during this five-year period, the IB will cancel the international registration accordingly. See TMEP §1902.09 for further information.

The holder of an international registration may request protection in additional Contracting Parties by submitting a subsequent designation. A subsequent designation is a request by the holder of an international registration for an extension of protection of the registration to additional Contracting Parties.

Each Contracting Party designated in an international application or subsequent designation will examine the request for extension of protection as a national trademark application under its domestic laws. Under Article 5 and Common Regs. 16 and 17, there are strict time limits (a maximum of 18 months) for the trademark office of a Contracting Party to refuse a request for extension of protection. If the Contracting Party does not notify the IB of a refusal within this time period, the mark is automatically protected. However, the extension of protection may be invalidated in accordance with the same procedures as for invalidating a national registration, e.g., by cancellation. See TMEP §1904.07 for information about invalidation.

The Madrid Protocol may apply to the USPTO in three ways:

Office of Origin. The USPTO is the Office of Origin if an international application and/or registration is based on an application pending in or a registration issued by the USPTO. Common Reg. 1(xxvi). See TMEP §§1902 et seq.

Office of a Designated Contracting Party. The USPTO is the office of a designated Contracting Party if the holder of an international registration requests an extension of protection of that registration to the United States. Common Regs. 1(xvi) and (xxv). See TMEP §§1904 et seq.

Office of the Contracting Party of the Holder. If the holder of an international registration is a national of, is domiciled in, or has a real and effective industrial or commercial establishment in the United States, the holder can file certain requests with the IB through the USPTO, such as requests to record changes of ownership (see TMEP §1906.01(a)(i)) and restrictions on the holder's right to dispose of an international registration (see TMEP §1906.01(b)). The expression "Contracting Party of the Holder" includes the "Office of Origin," as well as any other Contracting Party in which a holder is a national, is domiciled, or has a real and effective industrial or commercial establishment. Common Reg. 1(xxvibis).

1902   International Application Originating from the United States

This section covers international applications and registrations originating from the United States, i.e., international registrations based on an application for registration on the Principal or Supplemental Register pending in the USPTO and/or a registration issued by the USPTO on the Principal or Supplemental Register. See TMEP §§1904 et seq. for information about requests for extension of protection to the United States by the holder of an international registration originating in another country. International applications originating from the United States are processed by the USPTO's Madrid Processing Unit ("MPU").

MADRID PROTOCOL

The Protocol Relating to the Madrid Agreement Concerning the International Registration of Marks -- the Madrid Protocol -- is one of two treaties comprising the Madrid System for international registration of trademarks. The protocol is a filing treaty and not a substantive harmonization treaty. It provides a cost-effective and efficient way for trademark holders -- individuals and businesses -- to ensure protection for their marks in multiple countries through the filing of one application with a single office, in one language, with one set of fees, in one currency. Moreover, no local agent is needed to file the application. While an International Registration may be issued, it remains the right of each country or contracting party designated for protection to determine whether or not protection for a mark may be granted. Once the trademark office in a designated country grants protection, the mark is protected in that country just as if that office had registered it. The Madrid Protocol also simplifies the subsequent management of the mark, since a simple, single procedural step serves to record subsequent changes in ownership or in the name or address of the holder with World Intellectual Property Organization's International Bureau.

The International Bureau administers the Madrid System and coordinates the transmittal of requests for protection, renewals and other relevant documentation to all members. Source: USPTO

Chapter 4

WIPO · Madrid International Trademark System
How it works and Reproduction (Drawing) Rules

NOTE:
Source: Pages 120 through 137
The World Intellectual Property Organization (WIPO)
with the exception of pages
122 and 128 that are the author's

WIPO | MADRID
Madrid – The International Trademark System

The Madrid System is a convenient and cost-effective solution for registering and managing trademarks worldwide. File a single application and pay one set of fees to apply for protection in up to 122 countries. Modify, renew or expand your global trademark portfolio through one centralized system.

The Madrid System for the International Registration of Marks is governed by two treaties: the Madrid Agreement Concerning the International Registration of Marks, which dates from 1891, and the Protocol Relating to the Madrid Agreement, which was adopted in 1989, entered into force on December 1, 1995, and came into operation on April 1, 1996. Common Regulations under the Agreement and Protocol also came into force on that date. The Madrid System is administered by the International Bureau of the World Intellectual Property Organization (WIPO), which maintains the International Register and publishes the WIPO Gazette of International Marks.

Madrid System e-Services
Member Profiles Database Quick-Start Guide

Whether you're preparing an international application or managing your existing portfolio of trademark registrations, the Member Profiles Database gives you free access to the practices and procedures of Madrid System members across the globe.

WIPO IP PORTAL
Your gateway to the Madrid System, keeping you up to date on your trademark. Follow the status of your international application or trademark registration, access detailed information on all trademarks registered through the Madrid System, and keep an eye on competitors' trademarks.

Our new AI-powered, concept-based image search is now available. Choose the 'concept' strategy under image search to try it out.

WIPO
WORLD INTELLECTUAL PROPERTY ORGANIZATION

IP Services   Policy   Cooperation   Knowledge   About IP   About WIPO   🔍

https://www.wipo.int/portal/en/index.html

IP services

We provide IP services that encourage individuals and businesses to innovate and create.

Patents
WIPO | PCT
The International Patent System

Trademarks
WIPO | MADRID
The International Trademark System

Industrial Designs
WIPO | HAGUE
The International Design System

Appellations of Origin
WIPO | LISBON
The International System of Appellations of Origin

Dispute Resolution
WIPO | ADR
Arbitration and Mediation Center

Domain Names
WIPO | ADR
Arbitration and Mediation Center

https://www.wipo.int/madrid/en/

Madrid e-services

Search ⟩   **File** ⟩   Monitor ⟩   Manage ⟩

Global Brand Database

Madrid Goods &
Services Manager

Member Profiles
Database

Fee Calculator

International Application Form
(MM2) PDF

Madrid Monitor

Madrid Portfolio
Manager

e-Subsequent Designation
e-Renewal
e-Payment
Madrid System forms

WIPO Web-Site image, choose Trademarks, open to Madrid e-services.

How the Madrid System Works
The International Trademark Registration Process

The Madrid System is a convenient and cost-effective solution for registering and managing trademarks worldwide.
File a single application and pay one set of fees to apply for protection in up to 122 countries.
Modify, renew or expand your global trademark portfolio through one centralized system.

Stage 1

Basic application/ registration "Basic Mark"

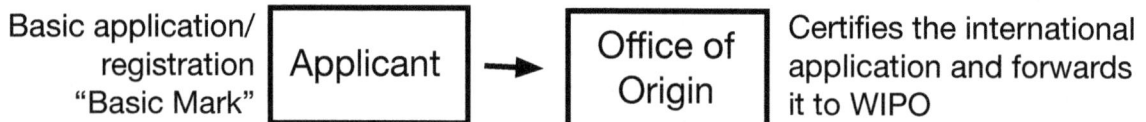

Applicant → Office of Origin

Certifies the international application and forwards it to WIPO

Stage 2

Formal examination; registers the mark in the International Register and publishes the international registration in the Gazette. Issues a certificate of registration and notifies the designated Contracting Parties

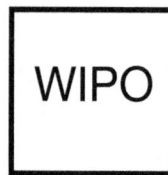

WIPO

Office of the designated Contracting Party

Stage 3

Scope of protection of the international registration will be determined by substantive examination under domestic law, within 12-18 months

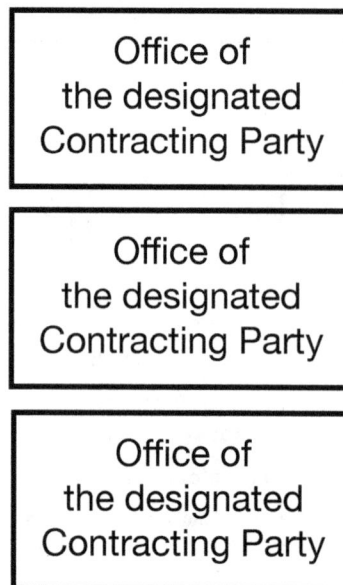

Office of the designated Contracting Party

Office of the designated Contracting Party

Studio 94 Graphic

Madrid e-services

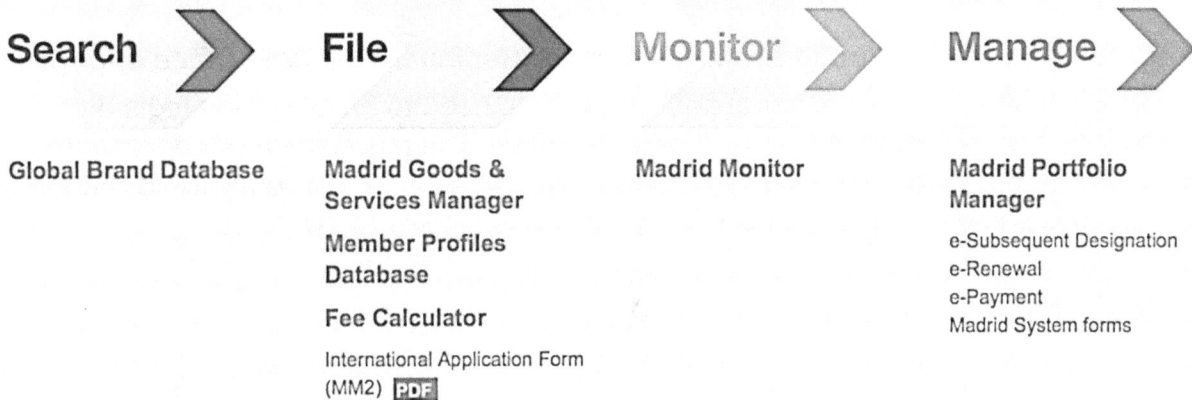

https://www.wipo.int/madrid/en/

Madrid e-services

Search >	File >	Monitor >	Manage >
Global Brand Database	Madrid Goods & Services Manager	Madrid Monitor	Madrid Portfolio Manager
	Member Profiles Database		e-Subsequent Designation
	Fee Calculator		e-Renewal
	International Application Form (MM2) PDF		e-Payment
			Madrid System forms

Search before filing
Before filing an international application, you should search to find out if identical or similar marks already exist in your target markets. Use this guide to find out how to search WIPO's Global Brand Database before filing your application, as well as how to locate the trademark registers of national and regional trademark Offices.

File an international application
In order to file an international application, you must have already registered or applied for a mark in your "home" IP Office. Learn more about the process, including your eligibility to use the Madrid System, how to complete your application form, required fees, and how to track the status of your application as it moves through the examination process.

Monitor an international application or registration
Once you've filed an international application with your "home" trademark office, it will be certified and sent to WIPO for examination. Learn more about the stages of the international registration process (including the roles played by WIPO and each national/regional trademark office) – including a preview of the types of documents you may receive along the way.

Manage your trademark registration
You can easily manage your international trademark registration through our centralized system. Find out how to renew or cancel, extend the geographical scope of protection, transfer ownership or appoint a representative, and learn more about the forms required for your requests.

Using the Madrid System

The Madrid System supports you throughout the lifecycle of your trademark, from application through to renewal. Use these guides to find out more about how to search for existing trademarks before you apply for protection, how to file an international application, and how to manage your international trademark registration.

Stage 1 – Application through your National or Regional IP Office (Office of origin)

Before you can file an international application, you need to have already registered, or have filed an application, in your "home" IP office. The registration or application is known as the basic mark. You then need to submit your international application through this same IP Office, which will certify and forward it to WIPO.

Stage 2 – Formal examination by WIPO

WIPO only conducts a formal examination of your international application. Once approved, your mark is recorded in the International Register and published in the WIPO Gazette of International Marks. WIPO will then send you a certificate of your international registration and notify the IP Offices in all the territories where you wish to have your mark protected.

It is important to note that the scope of protection of an international registration is not known at this stage in the process. It is only determined after substantive examination and decision by the IP Offices in the territories in which you seek protection, as outlined in Stage 3.

Stage 3 – Substantive examination by National or Regional IP Offices
(Office of the designated Contracting Party)

The IP Offices of the territories where you want to protect your mark will make a decision within the applicable time limit (12 or 18 months) in accordance with their legislation. WIPO will record the decisions of the IP Offices in the International Register and then notify you.

If an IP Office refuses to protect your mark, either totally or partially, this decision will not affect the decisions of other IP Offices. You can contest a refusal decision directly before the IP Office concerned in accordance with its legislation. If an IP Office accepts to protect your mark, it will issue a statement of grant of protection.

The international registration of your mark is valid for 10 years. You can renew the registration at the end of each 10-year period directly with WIPO with effect in the designated Contracting Parties concerned.

APPLICATION FOR INTERNATIONAL REGISTRATION GOVERNED EXCLUSIVELY BY THE MADRID PROTOCOL

OFFICIAL FORM MM2 – EXPLANATORY NOTES

> ### AUTHOR'S COMMENTS
> Form MM2 is the basic form (both paper & electronic).
> Although paper is being phased out, they still put the information in the Notes.
> Again, I have only included the rules that refer to the mark's
> drawings, reproductions and specifications on digital images.

When filling in forms, please note the following instructions:

• The form must be printed on one-sided, size A4 sheets;

• The form must be filled in legibly using a typewriter or other machine. Handwritten forms are not acceptable.

• Where the space available in any part of a form is insufficient, one or more continuation sheets should be used. On the continuation sheet, it is necessary to indicate "Continuation of item number ....", and the information must be presented in the same format as on the form itself. The number of continuation sheets used should be indicated in the box at the top of the form.

All the forms are available in the three working languages of the Madrid System (English, French and Spanish). However, where the form must be submitted through an Office, the filing language(s) acceptable to each Office should be checked first.

Item 7: The mark

(a) Place the reproduction of the mark in the square, exactly as it appears in the basic application or basic registration.

Therefore, if the mark in the basic application or basic registration is in black and white, so must be the reproduction in this box. Likewise, if the basic mark is in color, the reproduction in this box must be in color as well.

Where the mark is a non-traditional mark (e.g., a sound mark or a three-dimensional mark) the reproduction of the mark in item 7 should match the reproduction of the mark contained in the basic application or the basic registration. Thus, when the reproduction in the basic application or registration consists of, for example, a perspective view of a three-dimensional mark, a musical notation or a description in words of a sound mark, then this is what should appear in box (a). Reproductions of non-traditional marks may require a supplementary description in item 9(e).

Note: Non-graphical reproductions – for example, a sound recording of a sound mark cannot be included in the international application.

The reproduction must be sufficiently clear for the purposes of recording, publication and notification. If it is not, the International Bureau will consider it irregular and inform the applicant and Office of origin accordingly. Therefore, if several views have been used to reproduce the basic mark, a sufficient number of those reproductions should also be included to ensure the reproduction is clear.

It is not possible to modify the reproduction of the mark after the mark has been registered by the International Bureau.

The reproduction should be two-dimensional and graphical or photographic, and should fit within the box, which is 8 cm x 8 cm.

Finally, the reproduction may be typed, printed, pasted or reproduced by any other means, but note that the mark will ultimately be published in the Gazette in exactly the same format as it was presented.

(b) This box need only be used when color is claimed as a distinctive feature of the basic mark (meaning that it must also be claimed in the international application), but the reproduction of the basic mark in box (a) is in black and white because the Office of origin does not provide for publication in color. In such cases, the mark must be reproduced in color in box (b). The Gazette will then include reproductions of the mark, both in black and white and in color.

(c) Check this box if the mark is to be considered a mark in standard characters.

Generally, a mark in standard characters is equivalent to a mark consisting of a word or words, letters or numerals, or a combination of those elements. It does not include a stylized or figurative mark, or a mark depicted in a special style, font or color, rather than in a uniform style. It is not possible to add a claim that the mark is in standard characters after the mark has been registered by the International Bureau.

6 **PRIORITY CLAIMED**

☐ The applicant claims the priority of the earlier filing mentioned below:

Office of earlier filing: ....

Number of earlier filing (if available): ....

Date of earlier filing: .... (dd/mm/yyyy)

If the earlier filing does not relate to all the goods and services listed in item 10 of this form, indicate in the space provided below the goods and services to which it does relate:

....

....

☐ If several priorities are claimed, check the box and use a continuation sheet giving the above required information for each priority claimed.

7 **THE MARK**

(a) Place the reproduction of the mark, as it appears in the basic application or basic registration, in the square below.

(b) Where the reproduction in item (a) is in black and white and color is claimed in item 8, place a color reproduction of the mark in the square below.

(c) ☐ The applicant declares that he wishes the mark to be considered as a mark in standard characters.

(d) ☐ The mark consists exclusively of a color or a combination of colors as such, without any figurative element.

8 **COLOR(S) CLAIMED**

(a) ☐ The applicant claims color as a distinctive feature of the mark.

Color or combination of colors claimed: ....

....

....

(b) Indication, for each color, of the principal parts of the mark that are in that color (as may be required by certain designated Contracting Parties):

....

....

....

7

THE MARK

(a) Place the reproduction of the mark, as it appears in the basic application or basic registration, in the square below.

(b) Where the reproduction in item (a) is in black and white and color is claimed in item 8, place a color reproduction of the mark in the square below.

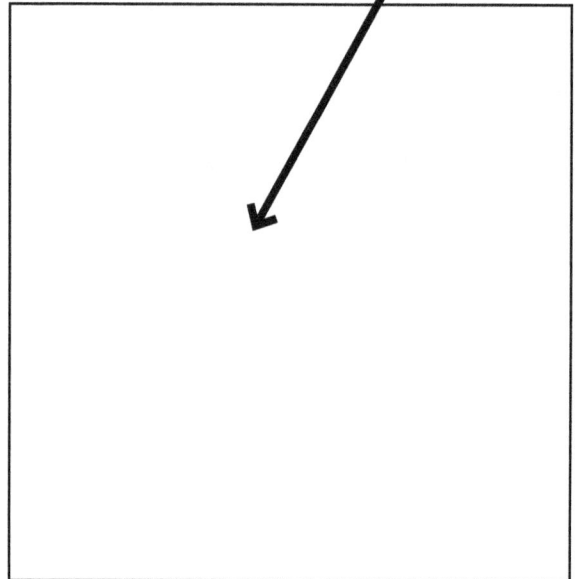

Pixel dimensions of no less than 250 or more than 944 (Example here: 855 x 851)

Image Width x Height

No less than 300 ppi & No more than 350 ppi (Example here 300 ppi)

Reference Material:
USPTO TESS Search
S/N: 76179959
Filling Date: Dec 12, 2000
Attorney: Robert J. Herberger

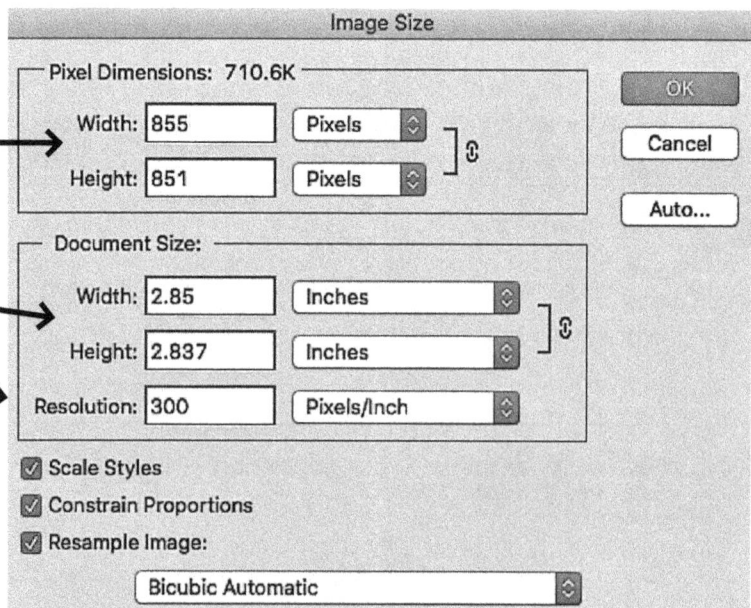

Image Size

Pixel Dimensions: 710.6K

Width: 855   Pixels
Height: 851   Pixels

OK
Cancel
Auto...

Document Size:

Width: 2.85   Inches
Height: 2.837   Inches
Resolution: 300   Pixels/Inch

☑ Scale Styles
☑ Constrain Proportions
☑ Resample Image:

Bicubic Automatic

Item 7: The Mark

46.　An applicant is required to provide a reproduction of the mark for which international registration is being sought, and this is the subject matter of item 7 of the form.

47.　The reproduction should be two-dimensional and graphic or photographic. It must be identical with the mark as it appears in the basic application or the basic registration. Thus, if the mark in the basic application or the basic registration is in black and white, so must the mark be in the international application. Likewise, if the basic mark is in color, so must be the mark in the international application.

48.　The two boxes in item 7 of the form measure 8cm x 8cm, which is the standard size for publication of the mark in the WIPO Gazette of International Marks (the Gazette). Where an applicant uses a self-generated form, the reproduction must still comply with these size parameters. That is to say, the reproduction of the mark must be of a size that would fit within a box measuring 8cm x 8cm.

49.　The reproduction of the mark should be sufficiently clear for the purposes of recording, publication and notification. If it is not, the International Bureau will treat the international application as irregular and will inform the Office of origin and the applicant accordingly.

50.　As to the format of the reproduction, it may be typed, printed, pasted or reproduced by any other means. This may often depend upon what is prescribed by the Office of origin. The mark will ultimately be published in the Gazette exactly in the format in which it has been presented.

51.　If the Office or origin has sent the application form to the International Bureau by fax, it will still be necessary to send to the International Bureau the original of page 2 of the form, bearing the representation of the mark. Please note that, in such case, only page 2 should be sent and not the entire application form. If the entire application form is sent in such case, it may be confused as a new international application. When sending the original of page 2 in the above situation, sufficient indications should appear to enable the International Bureau to identify the international application in question – for example, the number of the basic mark, or the Office reference number contained in the faxed international application. The Office should also sign the page 2 that is being sent. The Office should endeavour to ensure that the original of page 2 is sent to the International Bureau without delay, and preferably on the same day as the faxed international application is sent.

52.   A box at the bottom of item 7 of the application form is required to be completed by the Office in cases where the Office is sending the original of page 2 in the circumstances just outlined.

53.   Item 7 includes two boxes, side by side. In most cases, the representation of the mark will be contained in the left-hand box, numbered (a) on the form.

---

54.   A number of Offices do not provide for registration or publication in color. This is primarily the reason why the second box on the right-hand side, numbered (b), has been included in the form. The only situation when it will be necessary to utilize box (b) will be where color was claimed as a distinctive feature of the basic mark (and thus must be claimed also in the international application), but the reproduction of the basic mark in box (a) is, for the reason indicated above, in black and white. In such case, the mark must be represented in color also, and reproduced in box (b). The Gazette will then include representations of the mark in black and white, and also in color, for the purpose of establishing the scope of the color claim.

---

55.   If the mark is a non-traditional mark – for example, a sound mark, or a three-dimensional mark – the representation of the mark in box (a) that appears in the international application form should correspond with the mark as it appears in the basic application or the basic registration – it being understood that the representation must fit within the box in item 7 of the form. Thus, if, in the basic application or the basic registration, the representation of a three-dimensional mark is shown by a perspective view, that is how the mark should be represented in the international application form. If several views have been used to represent the basic mark, those representations should be included in the international application, up to a number such that the representation of the mark, within the box in item 7 of the form, will remain clear. If the basic mark is a sound mark, it may be represented in the basic application or the basic registration in the format of musical notation or a description in words. That then is how the mark should be represented in the international application form.

56.   These representations of non-traditional marks may require to be supplemented by a description in item 9(e) of the form. Non-graphical representations – for example, a sound recording of a sound mark – must not be included with the international application.

Mark in Standard Characters/Figurative Mark

57.   Item 7 of the international application form contains two boxes that may be checked by the applicant. The first of these is to indicate that the applicant declares that he wishes the mark to be considered as a mark in standard characters.

58.   Generally, a mark that is in standard characters will be equivalent to a regular mark that is a word or words, or letters or numerals, or a combination of those elements, as opposed to a stylised or figurative mark, or a mark that is depicted in a special style, font or color, rather than in a uniform style. A word mark that is in a stylised script would not normally be considered as a mark in standard characters. A mark that contains special characters or stylised elements should not be claimed as a mark in standard characters.

59.   The issue as to whether a mark is in standard characters is not always straight-forward because of the different indications, such as accents, which may be standard in one language and not in another. It is therefore entirely up to each designated Contracting Party to decide what is the effect of an indication that a mark is in standard characters.

60.   Where the box indicating standard characters has been checked and the mark is clearly not a mark in standard characters, the International Bureau will delete the indication of standard characters.

61.   In this regard, a mark consisting of, or containing non-Latin characters or non-Arabic numerals will not be considered by the International Bureau as a mark in standard characters.

62.   The International Bureau will assign a classification in accordance with the International Classification of the Figurative Elements of Marks (Vienna Classification) where the mark is not a mark in standard characters.

Mark Consists of a Color or of a Combination of Colors, as Such

63.   In many jurisdictions, a color, as such, or a combination of colors may, in itself or themselves, function as a trademark, to differentiate goods and services of one enterprise from those of another. It is important to distinguish between marks that consist of a color, or colors, as such, and marks that may, for example, be word marks or stylised marks, or other non-traditional marks, that happen to be in color, as against being in black and white.

64.   If an applicant wishes to file for the international protection of a mark that is a color, or combination of colors, as such, then he should place in box 7(a) a visual representation of the color and check box 7(d). An indication, in words, of the color(s) should also be given, in item 8(a). It will generally be required that the color or colors be indicated in a way that is clear, understandable, durable and easily accessible, and this is usually attained by the applicant indicating, by words, the color or colors in question, followed by a reference to an international color classification system, such as Pantone.

65.   If the applicant wishes also to provide a description in words for the color(s) applied to the goods or used in relation to the services that are the subject of the application for protection of a mark that is a mark in color, as such, this should be done in item 9(e), which provides for a description of the mark.

Color Claimed

66.   NOTE: the indication that the applicant claims color as a distinctive feature of the mark is not to be confused with a mark that consists of color, or of a combination of colors, as such (see above).

67.   Item 8 provides for an indication, in box (a), that the applicant claims color as a distinctive feature of the mark. A color claim means that the applicant considers the color or colors to be an integral or essential part of the mark. If color is claimed, the box in item 8(a) should be checked by the applicant to indicate that he is claiming color as a distinctive feature of the mark, and the applicant should also indicate, in words, the color or colors claimed. In item 8(b), the applicant can further indicate, for each color, the principal parts of the mark that are in the color or colors concerned. In fact, this is a requirement in certain designated Contracting Parties, where the international application includes a color claim.

68.   NOTE: in certain designated Contracting Parties, the very fact that the reproduction of the mark is in color will require automatically that color is claimed expressly, giving an indication, in words, or the color(s) concerned. In order to avoid receiving a notification of provisional refusal from such Contracting Parties, it may be advisable for applicants who are seeking protection for a mark that is in color(s), to include also in the international application a color claim by checking the box in item 8 and completing the remainder of item 8(a). Reference is made, for example, to Information Notice No. 4/2009, issued by the International Bureau (see paragraph 109 below) concerning designations of the United States of America (entitled Tips for Holders of International Registrations Seeking Extension of Protection to the United States of America: Avoiding Provisional Refusals) where a suggestion made by the USPTO was noted as follows:

> *"[...] The USPTO encourages the inclusion of a color claim whenever the mark is in color, along with an indication by words of the color(s) claimed and a description of where the color(s) appear(s) in the mark."*

69.   Please refer to paragraph 54, above regarding the inclusion in box 7(b) of a reproduction of the mark, in color, where the reproduction of the mark in box 7(a) is in black and white and the applicant intends to make a color claim.

70.   NOTE: if the mark contained in the international application is a color mark and the applicant does not claim color as a distinctive feature of the mark, that does not mean that the International Bureau will or may publish a black and white reproduction of the mark. The mark as published by the International Bureau will correspond to the mark that is in the international application, which in turn will correspond to the basic mark – that is to say, a reproduction in color.

Item 9: Miscellaneous Indications

Item 9(a): Transliteration

71.   Transliteration is not to be confused with translation. Where the mark consists of, or contains, matter in characters other than Latin characters, or numerals other than Arabic or Roman numerals, a transliteration into Latin characters or Arabic numerals must be provided. Transliteration is a phonetic representation of the mark in Latin characters, following the phonetics of the language of the international application. In simple terms, the mark, as it sounds, is reproduced in Latin characters. Transliteration is provided for in item 9(a) of the form.

Item 9(b): Translation

72.   Where the mark consists of or contains words which may be translated, it is advisable, where possible, to provide such a translation. Provision for translation is made in item 9(b) of the form. The translation may be into English and/or French and/or Spanish, irrespective of the language of the international application. The provision of a translation, at the option of the applicant, may forestall requests for a translation by the Office of a designated Contracting Party. The International Bureau will not check the accuracy of any translation of the mark, nor will it question the absence of a translation or provide a translation of its own.

Item 9(c): Mark that Cannot be Translated

73.   Where the applicant is aware that the word or words appearing in the mark cannot be translated (that is, they are merely invented or made-up words), this may be indicated by checking the box in item 9(c) of the form. This is intended to forestall a request by the Offices of designated Contracting Parties for translation. Obviously, it will be possible to complete either item 9(b) or 9(c), but not both in the same international application form.

Item 9(d): Special Type of Mark

74.   Where the mark is a three-dimensional mark, a sound mark or a collective, certification or guarantee mark, this should be indicated by checking the appropriate box in item 9(d) of the form. Note that such an indication may be given only if it appears in the basic registration or basic application.

75.   In the case of a collective, certification or guarantee mark, regulations governing the use of the mark are not required as part of the international application, and should not be sent to the International Bureau with the international application. A designated Contracting Party may, however, ask for such regulations to be filed. In order to forestall a refusal by such a Contracting Party, an applicant may wish to send the required documents directly to the Office of that Contracting Party as soon as he receives from the International Bureau the certificate of international registration.

Chapter 1300 - Service Marks, Collective Marks, and Certification Marks

The Trademark Act of 1946 provides for registration of trademarks, service marks, collective trademarks, and service marks, collective membership marks, and certification marks. 15 U.S.C. §§1051, 1053, and 1054. The language of this Manual is generally directed to trademarks. Procedures for trademarks usually apply to other types of marks, unless otherwise stated. This chapter is devoted to special circumstances relating to service marks, collective marks, collective membership marks, and certification marks.

AUTHOR'S COMMENTS

Chapter 1300 in the USPTO TMEP manual
is covered in Chapter 3 of this book

A word mark in a stylized script would not normally be considered as a mark in standard characters. Also, a mark containing special characters or stylized elements should not be claimed as a mark in standard characters.

The International Bureau will assign a classification in accordance with the International Classification of the Figurative Elements of Marks (Vienna Classification) when the mark is not a mark in standard characters, and the mark consists of or contains non-Latin characters or non-Arabic numerals.

(d) In many jurisdictions, a color, as such, or a combination of colors may be registered as a mark. A color mark applies to cases where, for example, the applicant wishes the color itself (e.g., a specific shade of red) or a combination of colors, to be the mark. This is different from cases where the mark to be protected consists of figurative elements or stylized characters that happen to be colored. In such cases, the correct name for the mark is a mark in color, not a color mark per se.

To protect a mark that consists entirely of a color – as a color mark per se – provide a description in words of the color(s) in question in item 8(a).

Enter a description in words of the color(s) in item 9(e).

Item 8: Color(s) claimed

(a) When one or more colors are considered to be an essential part of a mark and colors are claimed as a distinctive feature, check the box and describe (in words) the color(s) claimed. It is advisable to include a reference to an international color classification system, such as RGB or Pantone.

Note: A color claim is not a mandatory requirement in the international procedure. However, it may be a requirement in certain designated Contracting Parties. Therefore, to avoid any future refusals, it is advisable to check box (a) and provide the requested information.

(b) Use item 8(b) to further indicate the principal parts of the mark that are in the color(s) in question.

If the mark consists of multiple elements like a car, a flower and a cat, specify that "the car is green, the flower is red and the cat is brown".

Item 9: Miscellaneous indications

(a) Transliteration: When the mark consists of non-Latin characters or numerals other than Arabic or Roman numerals, a transliteration of the mark in Latin characters and/or Arabic or Roman numerals is required. This means, in simple terms, a phonetic reproduction of the mark as it sounds. The reproduction should be in Latin characters, using the language of the international application. It must not be confused with translation.

(b) Translation: If the mark consists of or contains translatable words, it is advisable to provide a translation into all three languages (English, French and Spanish) in item 9(b). Although this is not a mandatory requirement in the international procedure, it may be a requirement in certain designated Contracting Parties. The International Bureau will not check the accuracy of a translation, nor will it question its absence or provide any on its own initiative.

(c) If the words in the mark have no meaning and therefore cannot be translated, check this box.

(d) When the mark is a three-dimensional mark, a sound mark, or a collective, certification or guarantee mark and it appears as such in the basic application or registration, check the corresponding box.

Note: Do not send the regulations governing the use of a collective, certification or guarantee mark to the International Bureau. However, many Contracting Parties do require such regulations, so it is better to send them directly to the designated Contracting Parties so as to avoid a potential future refusal.

(e) Description of the mark: If a description is included in the basic mark, you may either include it or omit it from, the international application. In some cases, the Office of origin may require the same description to be included in the international application.

If the mark is not among the types listed under item 9(d), use this space to elaborate on the nature of the mark (e.g., hologram or motion mark). However, the description must still match the description in the basic mark.

Where the description of the basic mark is in a language other than the language used in the international application, a description should also be provided in the language of the international application.

The International Bureau will not check or question the accuracy of the description, or any translation thereof.

(f) Verbal elements of the mark: Providing this information is not mandatory. The International Bureau captures (from the reproduction in item 7) what appear to be the essential verbal elements of the mark and uses them for administrative purposes (primarily in notifications and correspondence). However, if the mark is in special characters, hand-written or contains verbal matter, the words or letters could be misinterpreted or it may not be apparent what should be captured. Therefore, it may be preferable for the applicant to indicate what he considers to be the essential verbal elements of the mark. Nevertheless, any such indication is entirely for information purposes and not intended to have any legal effect.

Note: If the box for standard characters in item 7(c) is checked, this item should not be filled in.

(g) To disclaim protection for any element of the mark, the element(s) in question should be indicated here.

This item is intended to avoid requests from designated Contracting Parties for any such disclaimer (for example, a disclaimer with respect to non-distinctive elements of the mark, such as "30 ml" or "Made in …"). Note that if a disclaimer is included in the application, it must be applicable to the international registration as a whole, not just to some of the designated Contracting Parties. It is not possible to include a disclaimer for elements of the mark after it has been registered by the International Bureau.

INDEX